In Search of the Truth

Dave Church

Order this book online at www.trafford.com
or email orders@trafford.com

Most Trafford titles are also available at major online book retailers.

Printed in the United States of America.

ISBN: 978-1-4269-4309-6 (sc)
ISBN: 978-1-4269-4310-2 (e)

*Our mission is to efficiently provide the world's finest, most comprehensive book publishing
service, enabling every author to experience success. To find out how to publish your book,
your way, and have it available worldwide, visit us online at www.trafford.com*

Trafford rev. 09/14/2010

Trafford
PUBLISHING®   www.trafford.com

North America & international
toll-free: 1 888 232 4444 (USA & Canada)
phone: 250 383 6864 ♦ fax: 812 355 4082

Biography of "In Search of the Truth"

When something stops or prevents the wonder of sexual intercourse in a marriage; what is it that seems to keep a man and wife together the same as if nothing happened? Or:

What is it about sexual intercourse that's so intense that if one of the partners starts "cheating" on the other; they almost immediately feel it the next time they have sex? Or:

What did Adam and Eve have between them, before they sinned, that gave God cause to tell us they only started having sex after they sinned? **"And Adam Knew his wife Eve".**

The first part of everyone's effort to answer these questions is that " it's got to be something spiritual"! That makes sense, because our questions deal with physical restriction; or with spiritual freedom. But that's also an answer which will satisfy no one! So here are the answers.

Our answer to the first question: is that in a truly successful marriage, sexual intercourse becomes so intense that not only is it the physical display of a love so great that we don't have enough or the right kind of words to express it: but when or if it's stopped, that lost physical expression of love just steps over into another form of **spiritual** expression. **And**: One of the first things Holy Ghost teaches a truly Born Again **husband**: (provided the husband is bright enough to ask): is that it's his responsibility to *intentionally* invite God into the "marriage bed"! God is not asked to come to the marriage bed as a spectator: (sex *isn't* a spectator sport): but God is invited to participate. That's the "secret"! And now **you** know it! A "three cord bond" is not easily broken!

But also: In those times when either one or both the man and wife are not Born Again; and there's a physical problem: their physical unity moves into their soul; and in their souls they find that completion. We've all heard of souls uniting in love. We'll also find deeper answers before this lesson is finished.

In order to answer the 2nd question, we'll answer the 3rd question next.

It's the firm belief of this author, and others, that although God did separate the body of the man in order to make a separate and distinct woman; and therefore also gave her a separate soul: (because a body without a living soul is just a zombie): God *didn't* separate their united spirit until *after* they sinned. In other words; and in order to have a perfect union: Adam and Eve shared the same spirit before they sinned. And by having a complete spiritual union, they were so satisfied they didn't need sexual intercourse to feel completed, or look for some other way to express their love.

That takes us to the 2nd question: where the answer is that because sexual intercourse is the physical **replacement** for ***lost spiritual unity***; the physical almost always becomes so intense that one of the partners will know when that *trust* is broken!

With these questions and answers in place; please know that it's the conclusion and opinion of this author, and study group, that virtually all sexual perversion has it's source and beginning in a search for the spiritual satisfaction and completion that was lost when Adam and Eve sinned! That's a "hot topic" and we're sure to get "flack", or maybe even directly aimed outbursts at us: but think about what we've said; and then speak out.

We've asked, and answered these questions, in order to show the straightforward and powerful insights the rest of our study is involved with. We don't hesitate to "tell it like it is"; because it's long past time to stop manipulating the truth!

We're also going to make this part of the biography of "In Search of the Truth" an entire chapter of our study later on: so look for more as we get to it.

There are also 2 specific and uniting threads that run throughout the entire study. One of them is the Truth about Jesus Christ! The other is our effort to advance information and revelation. It's also "fun" to try to see if these threads remain unbroken all the way through.

These several chapters are also some of the most difficult subjects we have to deal with today: but like the subject of sexual intercourse, the truth and insight that's brought out is seldom dull; hopefully interesting; and truly exciting because they're also subjects that are under the strongest satanic attack we know of. One thing we do promise; is that if this little book is truly studied, the reader is going to come away with far more information about "the end time" than they've had: and what they're going to know will be insights and information that isn't presently being taught or preached but by only a few!

These are also the kind of subjects a lifetime of family study has produced. Study that said no subject is immune to question and challenge. Studies where every time 2 or more of us got together we could feel the presence of Holy Ghost among us so intensely we almost saw Him; because we usually asked Him to participate.

But also; in those times spent with Holy Ghost; who's also Comforter, we learned more about Him than is generally known; because we can learn a lot about someone when we spend time in company with them--- no matter that Jesus did say Holy Ghost wouldn't speak of Himself. That insight into Holy Ghost is also something we share in this study.

Please note that this work is not intended to try to close "the generation gap": we may ask God to help us do that at another time.

The gap we *are* trying to close just a bit, is the gap between those who seem determined to stand upon what our "fathers" and their fathers taught, without advancing any more than they have to: and those who've tried to advance that knowledge as much as they can.

We've also found that through studies like this one, it's really a lot of "fun" to be a Christian and a follower of Jesus Christ: because virtually every picture we verbally paint in this study includes every one of us in one way or another.

May you be truly blessed as you study this book.

Dave Church

Preface:

Dear Christian Reader:

Surely anyone is welcome to study with us; but our usual class is composed of interested Christians. That's why the salutation.

Before I became a minister: as a Marine, and then as a 40 year semi-truck driver; I've spent my life among people who are called "Mr. Normal"; or "Joe Common". And so my work has been called 'common" by those who believe I shouldn't write or teach at all. In fact, one such Ph.D said he read 5 books a day, but my work was so simple he had "'trouble" understanding it. A lesson in egotism? Well maybe! At least he admitted reading my work.

My dad used to say that Ph.D meant "pilled higher and deeper": which shows the great gap between being educated in class rooms, and being educated in the class of "hard knocks". And which-ever kind of education one has is usually the education that's said to be the better one.

My level, or kind of education isn't the point! Whether or not you can understand what I'm trying to teach you is! But I do try to write as closely to "street language" as I can; because that's the language the majority of us used and heard as we were first being taught.

And if I have to break every rule of grammar, punctuation, and tradition in order to help you understand, I have no reservation whatever in doing it.

You surely don't have to agree with any of this study! But it's my conclusion that you should at least understand it before you make up your mind.

All we have to do is watch the news to understand that we live in an age where the most successful politician or business person is the one who can manipulate the truth better than someone else!

And those of us, who have to suffer the results, or pay the price in consequences from manipulation, aren't even being considered. But!

If we study the "tone" of the Bible, we'll understand that "Joe common" and Mr. Normal" have an awesome advocate in Jesus Christ: who came to; and always searches out "the common man" first! So:

That's the "truth" we're in search of as we study. Not only the truth that's given to and for the common man; but the truth that's advocated by Jesus Christ; no matter who's in search of it. But please note; as we said before:

Although we are in a sense working to close some of the "gap" between what's called "the common man" and the "highly educated": we're not intentionally trying to close "the generation gap": even though we'd surely like to.

The younger generation is just going to have to try to fit themselves into one or the other of the groups we're intending to inform.

In closing: Please be advises that there's **a lot** of new things, in the area of information, in this; and it's going to be a lot of "fun" to find them and search out the potentials and possibilities of them: but being a Christian is a lot of "fun" when we find the truth!

Your friend and fellow Christian

Dave Church

In Search Of the Truth

A Bible Study
By
Rev. Dave Church

John 14;

"I am the way, the truth, and the life: no man cometh to the Father but by me".

In Search of the Truth
By: Rev. Dave Church
Don't Just Read! Study!

Knowledge is power! Often, it's even greater power than money! And like money, the more knowledge one has, the more we seem to want. But the trap is that people can become so obsessed with the desire to gain more knowledge, they fail to properly act upon the power of the knowledge they have.

With "the age of the computer" upon us, everyone seems to think that all the knowledge that's ever existed can now be found. Many Christians also remember that this increase of knowledge is the fulfillment of a prophecy given in the book of Daniel. **We** just haven't considered, that knowledge about God is going to come to us in what we can only call "stages of progressive revelation". And we've been waiting for a sudden fulfillment of "God knowledge" similar to the fulfillment the computer gave. However!

Progressive knowledge: (which is also progressive revelations of knowledge): is seen in the fact that our "fathers" were "right and correct" in what knowledge they had, *"in their time"!* We are "right and correct": (*if* we've progressed ahead with the knowledge our fathers gave us): "in our time"! And our children; followed by our children's children; will also be right and correct "in their time"; if the world continues to stand.

Today with all the knowledge that's contained within the computer, and on the internet; it's easier to go to **it** than to try to learn through study. But that can get us into trouble!

Experience has taught us that sin prevents us from having a face to face relationship with Jesus Christ.

And so, the only real and true way to gain a working relationship with Him is to learn about Him through study and living experience.

In fact, we've found that the more we come to know about Jesus, the easier it is to Love Him. And to reach a point of intently---completely Loving Jesus, can bring us to a place of relationship many know almost nothing about.

For instance: Some might say that having spiritual insight is the same as having the gift of discernment. Not!! Spiritual insight is something any Christian can gain:

It comes with having a strong relationship with Holy Ghost; which comes with truly Loving Jesus.

It comes with "study to show thyself approved unto God; a workman that needeth to not be ashamed": it comes with "know the truth and the truth shall make you free"! And; we can't say it enough! It comes with learning to love Jesus Christ, through knowledge of Him! And:

It's through being given spiritual insight that we've come to find this truly awesome knowledge about what God is doing in these last days; as He brings "rapture closer and closer to those who are Born Again! We're not trying to take the credit for finding this insight! If Holy Ghost hadn't given it to us, we'd never have known it ourselves.

Now that we have the awesome and often powerful information contained in this study; we also have no option but to share it with people who may not know or understand what God has shown us. However!

There are many things that restrict our understanding; in many areas of study. And in "these last days", restrictions seem to cloud our minds even more: especially when we try to gain an understanding of subjects that we *know* are being manipulated by those in power. Even our news and historic documentaries *are* being manipulated to some degree!

Often with the intent of making "old fashioned" Christians look like ancient "fools" who refuse to progress with the rest of the world. We've commented on one of the problems with "closing the gap". But that's an internal problem! It hasn't changed the basic foundation that we teach is the "only" way to gain Salvation, and everlasting life with God. But again:

If we can gain the truly exciting relationship with Holy Ghost we spoke of; He will help us filter through mistakes and intentional lies that are our "daily fare" from the public forum.

God is long-suffering and extremely tolerant of Christian ignorance! He knows there's a lot of basic knowledge and understanding yet to be learned as Christians are led into "spiritual insight". And one of the better ways to gain new and deeper insight into God's word, is to intentionally spend time preparing one's mind to receive those things. With the power and authority of "Choice" in place; **never** fear that God is going to force anyone to change their mind and believe the new and deeper.

In this study, one of the "keys": (which really *isn't* insight; but which does lead us to understand what God is teaching): is if we have, or can gain, some knowledge about farming and growing things in the ground.

Jesus used the concept of planting and growing in most of His parables; because planting and growing is fairly easy to understand. That's why we're going to see terms like planting, harvest, and first-fruits, as we study these lessons from God.

There's an automatic blessing on those who study God's word. The blessing is that the Spirit of Christ Jesus: (Holy Ghost): is always available to those who will seek Him out for answers. Never overlook this advantage.

So now; we have before us at least an opening into the importance of **study** in God's word. We've been made aware of the fact that knowledge and information about Jesus Christ isn't going to be "handed to us" the way it is in the computer. And; hopefully, we have an insight into the potentials and possibilities that will come with advancing the knowledge we've been given by our "fathers" and teachers. But; as we've also shown" *never* overlook, or forget to use the power that's already available in what knowledge we already have; and what we've already established in study!

Born Again: What does it Mean?

In teaching and bearing witness of Jesus Christ through the years: we've been surprised at how un-knowing people are about what God does, when someone receives Jesus Christ and gains Salvation.

Many people just don't have; and/or they've never developed the ability to see things with their mind. All they have is a fairly limited ability to imagine. So they have to learn from those who do have this ability. So; maybe people can understand the things that happen when we're Born Again if we can explain it by using physical comparisons. By the way: this may just be the most important piece of knowledge we can gain in our entire life!

In the 26th and 27th verses of Genesis 1; God said *"let us make man in our image, after our likeness"*: Please note the use of the words "us" and "our": because it's clear that in a sense, God is talking to Himself! Not like we do; because we're each a singular individual. When God says "us" or "our", we've learned that it's *one* of the persons of God speaking to the other *two* persons of God. And at the time of man's creation; the *three* persons of God are "God the Father"; "God the *Word*"; and "God the Holy Spirit". Unique to all of creation, almighty God is actually and literally these 3 distinct persons. Each one of them declares "I am God", because they each one, are God!

So; at that time; by saying "let us make man in our image, and after our likeness"; God intended to make man, by following the "**pattern**" and "**form**" of how God is: *one being* composed of *3 persons*. And when God was finished making man; He had before Him, one complete human being, with 3 distinct **parts**! With each one of man's 3 parts corresponding to each one of the 3 persons of God

The soul of man corresponds to the person who is God the Father: who is also the central person in the God-head.

The body of flesh of man corresponds to the person who is God the Word: who is the only "flesh" of God earthly people will ever see. And who later on became Jesus Christ.

Because there's a 3rd person in the God-head; that means man must also have a 3rd part: which is a spirit; and which corresponds to God the Holy Spirit.

Hopefully, what we've been able to do, is explain the "make-up" of every human; and we really haven't had to step over into non-physical things very far to do it. But!

Holy Spirit is a person; a being as individually distinct and self aware as is either God the Father or God the Word. The form of His singular and entire being is **totally** non-physical however.

This may never be completely understood; but the very fact that Holy Spirit lives and exists demands that He live and exist in *everything* that exists.

From the stars and galaxies in our heavens to the very throne of Almighty God: if something is and exists, there also Holy Spirit can be found. We're going to find that Holy Spirit is "strange", even in heaven. And so; although we could spend page after page, trying to explain the existence of Holy Spirit: (and how He's different from Holy Ghost or Comforter): we wouldn't get any farther than we are right now: that makes it a good place to stop. The only point we need to make; is that in the same *way* that Holy Spirit "inhabits" all existence, our human and individual spirit "inhabits" all of our individual being---both our body of flesh and our non-physical soul.

So: Before Adam and Eve sinned, they each had a soul, a body of flesh, and a spirit: and note that all 3 of their parts were alive before they sinned! We need to look at the 17th verse of Genesis 2, and find God's warning against them sinning: ***"But of the tree of the knowledge of good and evil, thou shalt not eat of it: for in the day that thou eatest thereof thou shalt surely die".***

As we study the story, the Bible shows us that Eve was "beguiled": (tricked and lied to): into eating of the fruit of this "tree of knowledge" first. And then she gave it to Adam, who: (knowing what he was doing): **chose** to also eat of it. This is the "first" sin of man; and the "source" of all the "troubles" we have to work through and deal with our entire lives.

But yet; we know Adam and Eve "lived" for literally hundreds of years after that "day". Is God a liar when He said "in the day"? Not Hardly! Did He mean "eventually", as some would have us believe? Again, No is the answer. So what died? What fulfilled God's warning, "thou shalt surely die" Because we know that their bodies of flesh continued to live, we also eliminate their souls from dieing; because the evidence is clear that our soul and our "mind" are so closely united: (not our physical brain but what's produced in it): they might just as well be the same thing. So a body with a dead soul is nothing more than some kind of a Zombie. The answer then, is that it was the death of Adam's spirit part which died that instant. Please note: Before they sinned, God called the **union** of Adam and Eve simply "***Adam***". And by the way; that's an insight, and an answer into why people should stop trying to call God a chauvinist because there are so few women mentioned in the Bible. All the listings of the "begets" for example, are **both** the husband and wife; because through marriage God sees only *one unit*, which He chooses to call by the name of the husband.

We find in verse 7 of chapter 3, that *something* happened in Adam and Eve which showed them that their *spirit* had died:

"And the eyes of them both were opened, and they knew that they were naked; and they sewed fig leaves together, and made themselves aprons".

At this point however; we're going to stop the flow of information. Because; what comes next is not only the revelation of one of the most awesome "pictures" we can give in this entire study: it's something *every* scholar who's ever lived has simply "stepped over"! It's going to require an entire chapter to show it all; and to examine some of the things we've also missed because we missed this first picture. So we ask for patience until our study can take us to that picture and insight. And so:

Because Adam and Eve continued to live in their flesh; we go to the fact that it was their disobedience, and their "accountability" for this sin, that caused their spirits to die. And because of "genetic inheritance" this "seed of sin" has been passed into every human born from their union: *except one*!

Individual "accountability for sin": (even our inherited sin): is the reason our individual spirits cannot live! And when we become accountable; that's the instant our spirit dies within us! Please note:

Even though a newborn baby has done nothing to be held accountable for, every baby is born with this inheritance from Adam: (the first father of us all): which is Adam's "legacy" upon us. God tells us not to "blame him", because any and every one of us would have done the same thing. But when we're in the worst of stress and satanic attack, sometimes it's hard to not think bad about Adam. Also note: and this is even more important:

All the evidence available proves that this "genetic inheritance" from Adam is in our blood; made part of our blood; which; because our blood flows through every part of our flesh; is the reason sin permeates our entire body.

Jesus Christ is that "one exception"! He was born without sin: without this genetic inheritance. And we'll look at His credentials shortly. But, because there's a lot of misunderstanding and debate over how sin is in our flesh, and what it does; we need to allow God to explain it through us. Please have patience, and look closely at this; because it lays at the very core of the struggle between God and Satan.

The Bible declares: (in Leviticus 17;11): ***"For the life of the flesh is in the blood"***: And by reading the story of the sin of "Adam"; we know that they took the fruit of "the tree of the knowledge of good and evil" into their bodies. In other words; they bit into it; chewed; and then swallowed it. Through digestion, the chemicals and minerals of that fruit became a part of their bodies: in this case, and specifically, it became a part of their blood. Therefore: because there's only "one way" for a father to pass the genetic qualities from his body to the body of his children: (at conception): we understand that's how every one of us has "inherited" the genetic "seed called sin" into our bodies.

Romans 5;12 says it this way: ***"Wherefore, as by one man sin entered into the world, and death by sin; and so death passed upon all men, for that all have sinned:"***

Throughout the Bible, God makes a great "*fuss*" over the contamination of human blood! In fact: in Hebrews 9;22 he declares ***"and without shedding of blood is no remission"***!

Many have stepped over the word shedding, by not recognizing that it means "shedding **all,** and the **entirety**" of the blood that's in a body! We can understand that!

That it means "no blood is left in the body"! and because sin also goes out with the blood, and through deterioration as the body decomposes: it's also an example of the "old adage"; that "the operation was a success, but the patient died".

We'll understand this better, and expand it some, when we study the chapter titled "Death: the Doorway to Transformation".

Adam was not the father of Jesus!! Almighty God is His Father! And therefore when Jesus was conceived, the blood that formed in His body was uncontaminated. Please note:

The debate Satan & Co. have raised about the conception of Jesus Christ is certainly the most important point Christians can believe. Simply because Jesus was either conceived by the "overshadowing" of Holy Spirit, and Mary became pregnant that way; or else Jesus was a "bastard child" fathered by some nameless fool.

We also note: that it's scientifically proven that the blood of the mother of every baby does **not** intermingle with the blood of the baby: because there's a membrane within the umbilical cord, where it connects to the mother's uterus: (her womb): which is called the umbilical membrane; and which prevents that from happening.

In having this explained to us, by our sister Sarah Brown: (who was an R.N. for 35 years, and helped deliver over a hundred babies): her comparison is that this separation in the umbilical cord, is **similar** to the separation of the blood vessels in our lungs. There cannot be an unrestricted flow there, or else we'd drown in our own blood. Neither can there be a "free-flow" in the umbilical cord, because often times the contaminants in the babies blood can endanger and sometimes kill the mother.

Because this membrane kept the blood of Mary from intermingling with the absolutely pure blood of Jesus: and the blood disease of Joseph wasn't even allowed to become a part of the conception of Christ: that's what kept Jesus from inheriting any "seed called sin!! And the truly awesome fact, is that it's only the thickness of this membrane that's allowed God to provide Salvation to any and all who "call" upon the name of Jesus.

Going back and looking at the spirits of humans: please note:

There are 2 basic arguments over "when does our spirit die within us"? Both have so much merit that the argument probably won't be settled until Jesus settles it for us.

And since the argument doesn't cause much of a problem, both sides seem willing to let it stand. So: Let's look at both sides; so everyone can freely choose which side to agree with.

One side declares that because we "inherit" sin from our fathers; in exactly the same way we inherit any other genetic disease; or even our "blood line": we also inherit accountability! And with accountability, our spirit is already dead when we're born.

According to this point of view however, that's a conflict of terms; because it's contrary to the meaning of the word born. *It* means: "That which has; and/or has been given life? So, the use of the term "born dead"; which we'd have to apply to the human spirit at this time, is in conflict.

The other side argues that although we do inherit accountability: accountability *isn't applied* until we mentally develop and grow up to "the age of accountability": which they argue is when a child can be held responsible for their actions.

5

To them, the spirit of a baby is born *alive,* but dies at that age: (somewhere around 6-10 years old). Please note:

One thing that can open the door for a lot of answers, is the belief: (if it's true): that the spirit of a baby is born *alive!*

With a "living spirit"; there's no question about where our babies go if they die before the age of accountability. Both sides agree with the *fact* that our babies go **immediately** to heaven---carried on angel's wings!!! But having our spirit "born alive" is the only side with such an answer.

It can also be argued that if a person has some kind of mind disorder, but their spirit is still alive at birth, God could determine that they've *never* reached the age of accountability: accountability would then never cause their spirit to die. Also:

If a person lives their entire life, without ever hearing God's provisions for everlasting life with Him; God could also judge that that person hasn't reached the age of accountability either; because for anyone **past** the "age of accountability", they must know what the "wrong" they've done is; **and** the penalty; before they can be "judged" for it. The point is however:

When a person is judged: (by God and *no-one* else): to have reached the point of mental development where they are accountable for their sin; and they're at least aware that God has made alternatives available to them; the spirit of that person is *dead* at that point. And it will remain dead unless the person calls upon the name of Jesus Christ and receives Salvation!

And to "call upon the name of Christ Jesus" is to openly confess that they're a sinner; and believe within the heart of their being that Jesus paid their penalty for them: that's basically all anyone has to do.

God's part, is to enter into this person's dead spirit and give it *everlasting life*! In essence; that's all we have to know about being Born Again. But the subject of salvation is like a book with many chapters. We can spend our entire life in study of it; and still confess we don't know a 10th of what's right in front of us. Because this subject stretches from the day we're Born Again, all throughout eternity; it's seldom boring; often exciting; and shows the details of a living adventure that's greater than any book or movie!! And so:

Now we come to the time and place where we can show this truly awesome insight into some of the "deeper matters" of the Spirit. As we've just said; it's going to be an exciting adventure; most probably more "fun" than a movie!

Our Living Spirit

Genesis 2;25: *"And they were both naked, the man
and his wife, and were not ashamed."*
Genesis 3;7: *"And the eyes of them both were opened,
and they knew that they were naked; and they sewed
fig leaves together, and make themselves aprons."*

And now; we find an answer which a deeper study brings. But first; many haven't even thought to ask the question. So; the question is: "what was there about Adam and Eve's spirit that caused them to immediately take note when it died"? The answer is: that before they sinned: before they became accountable for their sin; the living spirit of Adam and Eve was so glorious and powerful that it actually worked and existed as a covering for their bodies of flesh! Their spirit literally lived outside of their flesh! That's the only reason they would have had to cover their bodies. And because things have changed, because of sin; when the spirit is alive within a human today, it's a covering only for our soul: it lives within our flesh now. It doesn't move outside of our body to cover our flesh when we're Born Again! So, please note:

If our opinion was sought; many of us might suggest to God that our dead spirits remain outside of our flesh. It would be a terribly sad thing to have to look at, if God answered us. But we'd at least know who is Born Again and who isn't! But again, that would take Faith out of the equation; and God wants us to live by Faith.

There are also several points of issue here; so please study with us as we look at as many of them as we can. We're only going to highlight the subjects: and not go into the details.

The first thing we note is that Adam and Eve were suddenly made aware of the fact that the glorious living spirit, that had covered them, was no longer there. If we can imagine how awesome was the glory of this part of them: (after all it came directly from the hand of God, and God said of His creation "it is good"): it's easy enough for us to see how shocked and stunned they were when it disappeared.

And they used Fig Leaves to cover their naked bodies: but this covering was "like an apron". That means they saw themselves naked only because the area of their "loins" was uncovered. Isn't that still true today? Don't we automatically cover this part with our hands when we're caught without clothes?

This also reminds us that when God made covenant with Abraham; the "sigh" and "seal" of that covenant was for every male in the House of Israel to be circumcised. Which can only be done if the covering and protection over this part of their body is removed. That's pretty "weak", even though it's true.

We do feel there's a correlation here; between Abraham and Adam; but as we said, we're not going to go into it in this study.

God's opinion is clear! In the use of Fig Leaves: that just didn't do the job! He used skins of an animal to make "coats" to cover their whole body. Again; covering their whole body and not just one area. And so:

The leaves from the fig tree became *man's* idea of a replacement for their glorious spirit. That's about as "weak" as it gets! It does remind us of a Bible story though; that's always seemed to be out of context; and no one has been able to give us clear understanding of why God put it in the Bible where He did. Because:

In Mark 11;12-14; and in 11;20-21 is the story about Jesus cursing a fig tree. The story is that one morning Jesus was hungry; and when He saw a fig tree some distance away it appeared to have fruit on it. When He approached though, the tree was only a pretend, without fruit. Jesus cursed it by saying ***"no man eat fruit of thee hereafter for ever".*** As they passed by it in the afternoon, the apostles were astonished that the tree was already dead at the very roots.

Is Jesus angry at the fig tree, because He's reminded of what Adam and Eve used the leaves for? Or is it from the fact that even His living spirit had to be concealed and hidden from display, on the inside of His body of flesh? Or is it that in Luke 21;29-36, Jesus taught that Israel is to be shown as a "type" of fig tree: putting forth its young branches, to indicate that the time is near for Israel to return to their land?

Any one of these pictures can be used to increase our knowledge about Adam's use of fig leaves to cover his nakedness. But there's another picture we'll only hint at by giving an insight. Which is: We don't know what the life-span of a fig tree is; but we can guarantee that it's *not* for-ever!

None of these pictures does much to increase our knowledge of the living spirit of Adam and Eve. Nor ours for that matter. We do want to return to that picture.

If we've used the evidence, and chosen to believe that even today the spirits of humans are alive when we're born; we also have a "sense" or a "feeling" that this part of us has an almost indescribable glory, "aura' and beauty about it. Not that we're trying to declare that our spirit is greater in glory than our body of flesh or our soul: (they each have their own particular glory):

But because it's beyond our ability to use words of explanation or description, we are the ones who look upon our own spirit as being something that's just totally awesome to behold. And then----

After the excitement of our "new birth" begins to wear off, and we start to study what it is and what's happened to and within us; we can't help but begin to feel that something even greater has happened to our now *living* spirit.

We feel that its greatness and glory is even farther beyond describing than it was before; because it's the one, and only, part of us that's been transformed from life to death to life again. And we'd like to be able to share the mind picture we have within us; but we just don't know how. Our conclusion is that it's only because this subject is still so "new" that we have a problem. God's word will help us, if we look in the right places; and as this message is spoken more and more our mental pictures will be easier to describe. And also:

In more than one place, Jesus is called "the second Adam"! But because we don't know what the first Adam even *looked like*; we have a problem with what to do with this declaration about Christ. But now that we have a place to start, we can begin to form a picture of God's intent for the first Adam, by looking at some of the things we know about this second Adam.

There's a story shown in all 4 gospels: but Matthew 17; 1-3 is the better picture of what's called "the mount of transfiguration". It's where Jesus was transfigured before the apostles Peter, James and John" and in which He was seen in company with Moses and Elias: (which is another name for Elijah). The description of a transfigured Jesus is fairly short: declaring only that His face did shine like the sun, and His raiment was white as light.

Just this much of a description, is enough for us to form a mental picture of Jesus standing before these men in a brightness and whiteness that was almost too glorious for them to look at. But the point we're being led to see, is that in *this* "transformed" state; Jesus is being a **portrait** of Adam before he sinned: and how he would have continued to look if he hadn't. That's Glorious!! However:

Because we have an established pattern now before us: we can satisfy ourselves that many of the mental pictures we have of Jesus are examples of Adam; as he was supposed to look. But:

There's a descriptive picture of Jesus: where Jesus is described as Jesus Christ, and no one else. Within this picture, surely we *will be* able to find **every one** of the positions of Jesus: Son of God: Son of man: Lamb of God: Messiah: Lion of the tribe of Judah: King above all Kings: and many others. But in Revelation 1;12-16, the apostle John does an admirable work of filling all these pictures and positions of Jesus Christ; while describing just one person!

Our point at this time is this: We've said it more than once already; and it's up to the individual to choose: but we now have two awesome pictures of Jesus: at Transfiguration; and at the isle of Patmos. John declares this about Jesus---**and us**, in 1st John 3;1&2: *"Behold, what manner of love the Father hath bestowed upon us, that we should be called the sons of God: therefore the world knoweth us not, because it knew him not."*

"Beloved, now are we the sons of God, and it doth not yet appear what we shall be: but we know that, when he shall appear, we shall be like him; for we shall see him as he is."

Again it's a choice: but we might like to underline the words "shall be like Him!

That's a promise! It's also in the form of a prophecy; because it's declaring a fact that will be in the future from John's writing. It's also one of those promises and declarations many of us have "trouble" with, because what God says doesn't fit with what we think of ourselves: or what we expect our place in heaven to be. But like the other positions and qualities God declares He "credits" us with; it's really hard to debate against words as simple as "shall be like Him"! But please also note:

As Jesus is shown in both these pictures: (the mount of transfiguration, and the isle of Patmos):we can have no doubt but that His Living Spirit not only resides as a part of Him, but it also resides on the outside of His body of flesh! Therefore---so must our spirit.

A Personal Note: about Our Living Spirit

In the preface of this work, as an author I said that if it would aid you in understanding: I'm willing to break any and all the rules of grammar, punctuation, or even tradition.

This is one of those special times.

We don't do it often enough; but there are times when a Christian needs to say "this is what I believe---this is why I believe what I believe"! So:

In the 15th chapter of 1st Corinthians; from verses 33 to verse 50, Paul is detailing the lesson about resurrection from the dead. In verse 40 he says; *"There are also celestial bodies, and bodies terrestrial: but the glory of the celestial is one, and the glory of the terrestrial is another".* And in verse 44 he declares; *"It is sown a natural body; it is raised a spiritual body. There is a natural body, and there is a spiritual body."*

When these two verses are combined with the fact that Scripture not only shows resurrection for all the Born Again dead: (at rapture): but also shows resurrection for the entire House of Israel: (from Abraham all the way to the Second coming of Christ): celestial and terrestrial: natural bodies and spiritual bodies take on an entirely different meaning from how they've been taught.

That's the "body of evidence" that leads me to believe as I do.

I've concluded that when God makes a "New heaven and earth", the House of Israel will have the same earthly "dominion" God gave Adam and Eve, over the earth.

Therefore; Israel will be resurrected into the terrestrial and natural bodies: while we are destined to have a home not of or on this earth; which causes us to be resurrected into the celestial and spiritual bodies.

That being true; it puts all the members of the entire House of Israel eternally having bodies "like" Adam before he sinned; and "like" the body of Jesus on the mount of transfiguration. While we; who are now "the

Body of Christ", destined to become "the Bride of Christ", will have bodies "like" the awesome and almost fearful body Jesus displayed to John.

This isn't something anyone needs agree with; because choice is complete. It's what this author believes though, and intends to stand on, unless Jesus changes my mind!

The Union of Sexual Intercourse

In our biography of this study, we showed our boldness toward the truth about sexual relations; and promised more. Here's more!

At it's basics and probably as it begins, it's our conclusion that *all* sexual perversion begins as a search for and a substitute for the real: the true: and the perfect experience! And because even the greatest sexual experience a husband and wife can have is a *lesson* in the fact that sexual intercourse is still a "**step down**" from perfection; this part of our lesson is intended to show us what that perfection is that we've stepped down from. The first problem is that there's no ***perfect substitute***!! For sure there's not a substitute for the sexual union: (which is perversion): but neither can we find a perfect substitute for God's perfect *spiritual* union: because sin, and man's own ignorance gets in the way. That's why things are as bad as they are; and we're inundated with sexual innuendo in speech, and in pictures that we wouldn't **not** look at even if we thought about it. Even the Muslim effort to be totally opposite to the "modern" countries like the U.S., Great Britain, or Australia: (to name a few): by forcing their women to cover up completely; is sexual perversion---and not religious decorum! If we don't believe that; look back at the history of America, when the "fashion" of the time was dresses that had the hem dragging the ground. It's said that men were "excited" by the display of an ankle. Wow!! But we're not going to explain *our* opinion, because it's all still a matter of choice.

The "real thing", as far as sex between a husband and wife is concerned, is the lesson God gives the husband in his position as "head of the family": and the one whose position declares that he goes first in the work of establishing equality under God with his wife. Please note:

No matter how we present this chapter; some are so "bitter" about the way things have turned out, we'd have to write another entire book to explain everything we're trying to show.

There's one point we do need to make about the husband's position as "head over"; which **God** established. Because she was proven to be vulnerable, and was "beguiled"; God set the husband in a position to "over-rule" his wife; for her own protection. His obligation, or duty to over-rule was for those times that she did, or started to do things that took her our from under his "protective umbrella". In other words; if a man saw his wife start to do something his experience or knowledge told him would cause her to be vulnerable to satanic attack; he has; or had the command from God to warn her against it: and to tell her why! Please remember: the man was "not deceived"!! That's all gotten lost somewhere through the years; as men just started letting "the law" do the work for him.

But in reality, and apart from the man's obligations before God, it was also his obligation to maintain and insure joint partnership and equality with his wife! O, how we've messed *that* up!

The husband holds an obligation of talking with his wife about **inviting** God into their "marriage bed" as a holy partner: which we've found few do; and loose an awesome blessing by that failure. But for those who know; the sooner the better.

And more than just following simple tradition and natural instinct, where the male is the aggressor and seeker; *the husband* must be aware of what things bring fulfillment to their union, and quickly discard those things that don't. The fact is: because it's "equality"; neither partner should feel it necessary to do something, or anything, just to "please" their partner unless they choose to do so. But communication is one of the "key's" to fulfillment.

But neither is it that the only thing the wife has to do is to make herself available to her husband, so she "satisfies his needs"; and fulfills her "wifely duty". The times when a wife supposedly thought about "canning peaches" or taking a trip while her husband sought "relief" is something that probably never was anyway. But again: ignorance over what God has given us sexual intercourse for; can bring down a marriage faster then any headache. And real---true understanding can build an intimate and private relationship between them that extends far beyond the marriage bed.

Have we ever felt the discomfort of being what's called "a 3rd wheel": when we seem to be left out of every little gathering or clique? If we all understood what God wants us to use the union of marriage for, every union would make any of us feel that way: because we'd see the intimate looks: the constant awareness of where their partner is: their personal language; both "body language" and spoken: if we don't have it ourselves, we'll even be a little jealous and wonder "what do they have"? and "how do we get it"?

If we all understood the lesson; we'd see the silent testimony of it in the fact that we'd be far less likely to see the men gathered in separate groups; while the women set around in the kitchen, or some other place separate from the men.

But what is it God is trying to teach us, that now shows us no matter how powerful or fulfilling sexual intercourse is; it's still a "step down" from that perfection we seek? The answers lay in the chapters and insights we've just seen: about the living quality of our individual human spirit; which Holy Ghost has brought to life within us through gaining Salvation.

As we've said, we all have differing degrees of difficulty in mentally "seeing" our living spirit. **We've** tried to explain where it comes from: and what it is. We're still at a loss to understand how it works however.

Like the "strangeness" of Holy Spirit, our human spirit is different from our soul---even though both are non-physical parts of us.

So, we're trying to limit what things we might think our spirit does, and relate the working power of it to just this one subject; because our spirit does so much it's easy to get side-tracked into other things. As a Born Again husband and wife are suppose to, we're going to try to follow the "pattern" God shows us.

As we've said the human spirit of Adam and Eve remained as one spirit in them, before they sinned. And because of that union of spirit, what they had was beyond sexual intercourse; but their choices brought that union down. But:

With God as the 3rd cord in our "3 cord bond", this step down from that perfect union *can be* as fulfilling and complete as any "less than perfect" *substitute* any has ever experienced. Please note:

We have no evidence of anything physical happening to Adam or Eve, other than the corruption and pollution of their flesh by sin. So; we also conclude that before they sinned, there was nothing actually preventing them from having intercourse. Our lesson is that they had this spiritual union so much greater than intercourse, that they just didn't need it to be fulfilled and complete in it. There's another lesson here; we're just going to have to wait to see it.

We've used the story of Abraham and the "rich man" for several analogies. This surely will be the most unusual.

In the story, Abraham and the rich man "*talked*" back and forth across the chasm fixed between them. And Yet! The earthly bodies of both of them was dead and buried in the ground. How did they communicate!

With their spirits dead, the **only** other option is that it's possible for one soul: (one mind): to communicate with another: especially when there's nothing left to talk with.

The reason we've gone into this story, is because when a husband and wife have a union that's "*almost as good as it gets*"; they sense and feel that same kind of mind to mind union; as though every part of their being is joined. And we're firm in our conviction that when all the restrictions are removed: when we all have a "New Body": communication will be more than just sensing or feeling! Through study, we're fully "persuaded" that in our eternal future, we'll all be able to communicate with one another using each one of our 3 parts! And we won't have to have sex to do it. (No; don't go there)

In a fashion, we've sort of "let the cat out of the bag". Because the one thing we've shown in this entire chapter, is that apart from "making babies"; it's all about communication!!

Sex is communicating love, honor, appreciation and gratitude; just to name a few in a long list of good things. Speaking is communicating the things we've yet to be able to do with our mind or soul

. But uniting one living spirit with another: (when the time comes and we can do it): is uniting *all* of our 3 part beings into an ability to communicate not only thoughts and speech, but to add the fullness of *emotion,* which is the only other missing part; and which can't be given to another right now without outwardly displaying it.

Adam and Eve were able to communicate *perfectly* because they had a living spirit they shared. We will share our spirit with Jesus Christ, and have that same kind of communication, through and with Him, and with one another! But, that's not all of it! Oh no!!

When Jesus Christ is married to "the Bride of Christ"; we have every reason to believe He's going to be a "perfect" husband. That means one of the first things He's going to do, is talk with His wife, and then intentionally invite the Spirit of God into our union, in order that *we* have another "3 cord bond"! Please note:

Because there are literally millions and millions of people who will make up the Bride of Christ; it's only the sin of our being that gives us thoughts like "is there going to be sex in heaven"? And none of us are bold enough to ask the question; even if someone just might have a correct answer! And while we're on the subject: the answer is---if sexual intercourse between a married and Born Again husband and wife is a "step down" from the perfection that God has available: which Adam and Eve shared before they sinned: what we're *going to have* in heaven is so awesome and tremendous: so *perfect* because the Spirit of God is involved: it would most likely kill a natural human of today.

But no matter what it's going to be; or be called: the absolute perfect Spiritual union of Jesus Christ and His Bride, is still going to be perfect communication, which results in perfect fulfillment!

Death: The Door-way to Transformation

The focus of the living is almost totally upon things of our physical life: on physical, visible things! If we'd wake up to that fact; we'd see that this obsession is the cause for many of our mistakes and ignorance in understanding non-physical things.

In speaking on the subject, Jesus said "that which is born of the flesh, is flesh: and that which is born of the Spirit is spirit". When we apply the dictionary meaning of the word "born" to that statement, we get a clearer picture. Once again: "Born" means; "to have; and/or to have been given *life*".

So every study of "what is flesh"; or what is physical"; is going to take us from all the way into the galaxies and stars of outer space, down into the substance of the smallest atom. And every study of Spirit or spiritual things; will take us all the way from the non-physical spirit that's within every one of us; through the non-physical world around us; all the way to God's throne in heaven. But just because our physical senses are dominant within us; and we have to "work" to look into the non-physical universes; that doesn't mean the non –physical is non-existent or imaginary. The best way we've found to explain it, is that in the same way we can look around at our physical/flesh universe, full of things and beings: so too can we find the non-physical universe of the Spirit filled with things and beings. Things of the Spirit; are things that are of and from different dimensions, or worlds, or even planes of existence: as some choose to call them: but which remain un-seeable to our physical senses. Some may tell us we have to use "imagination" to see these worlds.

But our conclusion is that instead, we use our human only ability to "see with our mind": Because seeing with our mind makes these things more real, than just imagining them. And its "human only" because we have no evidence that any animal apart from man, has "abstract thinking".

There may be as many different dimensions, or worlds, or planes of existence, as there are different galaxies in our heavens. But for the sake of this lesson, we need to focus only on 3 of them: our dimension of flesh and physical things: the dimension of non-physical things and beings that immediately surrounds our world: and the non-physical dimension of God's world.

In God's world we'll also see the objects and things that **declare** God: things that exist only because God exists. Surely, there will be many things we won't understand when we get to heaven. But we'll know what they're for, when it's explained to us by one of the inhabitants of God's world. Probably in the same way they were explained to the apostle John when he wrote Revelation. Can we even begin to look with our mind and see an angel of God giving us a "tour" of heaven? That's "gonna" be a "hoot"!

At this day and time; and limited specifically to people who are Born Again: there's only one way for a human to **permanently** go to God's heavenly dimension! That way is for us to **die** in our body of flesh. Then we're promised that *"to be absent from the body is to be present with the Lord"*. And every bit of evidence we have: (concerning those who are "un-saved"): tells us that when they die, they **immediately** go to hell. Please note:

The fact that all the un-saved go straight to hell; is why we also reject any idea or effort that's supposed to give them a way *out* of hell. Because--and this is *very* important!

The work of Jesus Christ is designed and intended to keep people from having *to go* to hell: it *isn't* intended to help people escape hell once they've chosen to go there!! That's also what makes the physical death of a person so important; because it "locks in" whichever choice they've made during their life. It's why we hold to the security of Salvation so strongly! Because: if we also believe there's been at least one time in their life that they've confessed Jesus Christ; in the presence of at least one truly Born Again Christian, who can "bear witness" of that confession; that one time is enough! It *will* provide them with everlasting life with God!

After that; the problems so many of us have, are from having a lack of knowledge. And most of that can be fixed.

As we've noted before: In 1st Corinthians 15;50 Paul declares *"Now this I say, brethren, that flesh and blood cannot inherit the kingdom of God; neither doth corruption inherit incorruption"*. The very first thing we need to show about this verse, is that it's a *demand* for transformation.

Transformation is the only way to change that which is corrupt into that which is incorrupt! And transformation is the ***only way*** to separate our flesh from our blood, and still keep the usable parts of our flesh alive. That's what the first part of this verse is telling us: that flesh and blood---in combination and union together---cannot inherit God's kingdom! Our "New body" **will** inherit---after it's transformed! Our blood is of **no use** to the kingdom of God---because it already has all the blood it needs---from Jesus Christ! Our blood is totally polluted anyway; by sin! But we still need to study about God using death to transform.

In John 12;24 Jesus said ***"Except a corn of wheat fall into the ground and die, it abideth alone: but if it die, it bringeth forth much fruit".***

Those of us familiar with farming: with planting and growing things in the ground: are more familiar with "increase" than may be the rest of us. But the subject is fairly straight-forward.

When we want to grow a field of corn, we *don't* plant an entire ear of corn. If we did, we'd end up with an unusable mess that won't produce anything. Because; the way this "system" works, is that one grain of corn, will produce one ear of corn. One grain of wheat or barley will produce one entire stalk, with many grains on it.

In fact: on the average, one grain of corn, producing one ear of corn, will produce about 300 grains of corn on the ear. That's not "fixed in stone"; but numbers give us an *idea* of the increase. In this case; one grain is multiplied 300 times. That means the new ear of corn is 300 times greater than the grain of corn that was planted. That's not fixed in stone either, because different kinds of growing things will produce different numbers.

An apple tree: grown from one apple seed: might produce more of less than 300 apples each year. But the one apple tree will normally produce thousands of apples over it's life time. So:

We now have at least a foundation upon which to establish the "multiplication of transformation"! The basic principal is also the same; whether we're looking at growing things in the ground or looking at humans who die in Christ Jesus. And please note:

Only through the work and sacrifice of Jesus Christ, can humans be transformed at all. Human transformation is likely to be found today *only* in those who are Born Again: and those who die without the judgment of "accountability" laid upon them. God knows!!

In the 1st chapter of Revelation, John describes Jesus as we're going to see Him. This is the picture of "the King of Kings": "the lion of the tribe of Judah": "Messiah to the house of Israel": and "Husband to the wife of Christ". By the way: if the husband is this glorious; can we even begin to imagine what God is going to make His Wife look like?

As our mind begins to give us a picture of what Jesus looks like; this description of His living Glory actually begins to cause fear and at least some nervousness to rise up in us. As has been said many times by the unsaved; "this is a picture of the guy you'd least like to meet down a dark alley"! And because it's our flesh that's dominant: totally corrupted by sin: we really have to "work" to control our rising fear of Him.

When we're "in" Christ, He's surely the best friend any of us could ever want! But our flesh; our "human nature" is in enmity with Jesus because of the sin that's in us: which is why we have such inner conflict. Two of our living parts struggle to get closer to Jesus: the other part tries to flee from Him. This is another reason God has to transform our flesh! Causing that which is corrupt to be transformed into that which is incorrupt. And then, our entire being will be in harmony with Christ.

The transfer of a person: from life to death to life again is what we're calling the transformation of people. Surely we'll not only see it happen; we'll participate in it personally, at the event we call "the rapture". We also believe this is the time Jesus will give us all our "New Body"; because when He comes to claim us from the earth, the Bible declares "and His reward will be with Him". Please note.

Hopefully we've already established that contrary to what many people seem to assume; this transformation is not going to suddenly also give us all knowledge; all power, and all ability! Like it or not, we're going to have to do some "study" when we get to heaven. In fact, there's *a lot* of knowledge we're going to have to learn, adjust to, and correct! But hopefully we've given enough information for us to also understand that with the mind restriction removed, we'll surely be able to learn the Truth a lot quicker than we do today.

A lot like a study on the subject of Salvation; study of transformation is as deep and lengthy as we choose to make it. In fact; the pictures of transformation are far older than Salvation: because we're totally convinced that as the Bible shows us "the Lamb slain from the foundation of the world"; that was the ***first work*** of Transformation!

The Lesson of Harvest

The Bible is our teacher here: and no one can say they have an "exclusive" insight into this lesson. Neither can we say that any one of us is the final authority on this subject. In other words; it's impossible to claim "copyright"; or even originality for this part of our lesson. However; it's only by learning this "lesson of harvest" that we come to understand the insight into one of the most important things God is going to be doing, in this time we call "the Great Tribulation". This "Tribulation" is the "end time" spoken of: the time of "God's wrath": "Jacob's trouble": and "Daniel's 70th week"!

The *background* of "the Great Tribulation" is given in the book of Daniel: chapter 9 and verses 24-27. And what Daniel is telling in chapter 9 is that through study he found that although the prophecy of time is stated as 70 weeks; it's actually 70 weeks of years; or 490 total years. And in verse 24 he gives a list of the things that will be accomplished during this 490 year span.

Surely; just about every Christian: (and most of the "unsaved" it seems): has been taught that after 69 of these weeks is finished: 483 years; Messiah is "cut off". And when Jesus died on Calvary; that was the "cut off" of those years. One of the better descriptions we've heard: is that like the picture of a great "stop-watch"; at the beginning of these 70 weeks of years, God pressed down on the button of this great clock, and the time of 70 began to count down: 69;68;67; etc. But after 69 weeks had been counted off; and at the death of Christ; God pushed the button down again, and the count-down stopped: leaving 1 of the weeks of years: 7 years; remaining. And so The first thing we find is that "Daniel's people" don't have to accomplish the entire list of things in the last 7 years: they only have to finish them!

So also note: One of the very important things we should keep in mind for these last 7 years, is that although Messiah has been cut-off; and now sits in glory at the right hand of the Father; the things yet to be done, should have been done, and were suppose to be done; while He was physically present on the earth.

This is a "key" and an insight into especially "the 4 horsemen"! Because they come to earth actually in **representation** of Jesus Christ!! In f act; we could gain a lot, in understanding Revelation: if we'd study it from that perspective: of Christ Jesus literally being on the earth.

The 26th and 27th verses of Daniel 9; show that a "prince" shall come, and "confirm the covenant with many for one week". The day this "agreement" is signed and noted, it becomes evidence of the fact that many in Israel will also return to the "old way" of sacrifice. And then, God's thumb will press the button of that great stop-watch once more; and the count-down will resume!

Knowing we would see the return to animal sacrifice in the Jerusalem temple if we were still here when it started, is surely the strongest reason many Christians have concluded that the Born Again cannot be on the earth when Tribulation happens. Because; if we were here; and saw this beginning, it would *then* be possible for us to count the days; to the day of "the abomination of desolation" for instance. The days of the events of Revelation in fact could be counted to the very day in which Jesus Christ will return to earth as Messiah. Because all these numbers of days, months, and years are given in prophecy! *None* of these are days we're suppose to know however! And it would be a *violation* of the words Jesus spoke: (no man may know the day or hour): if we did: which would make Him a liar! So: we back up! And declare the obvious!

That everyone who is Born Again will not---***can not***---be on the earth when this agreement is signed! For us; that means that the day we call rapture must come to pass before the count-down of tribulation begins! Again, please note:

In all the things we're seeing here; the concept of "time" seems to underlie it all. And not just a generalization of time; but precise time: time divided down into years, months, and days. After all, most of these events have been eons in building: some even going back before the time of man on earth. The attitude of most has been that God is going to take as much time as He needs, to get these things accomplished. But in this time of Tribulation God seems to turn it completely around, by setting a tone of precision and even haste on the events. Beginning with the first event, which will set off this chain of events; and which will probably be either the rapture of the Born Again; or the invasion of Israel by Gog and Ma-gog: it's as if God is warning Satan & Co. that they only have this number of days or months to prepare a response. Even in the 20th and 21st verses of Revelation 9; we're shown that those who haven't been killed by the plagues won't repent of their sins. And we've made this "a note", in order to say that it's simply beyond reason or understanding to explain why people would be so forcefully against God!

Returning to the lesson of harvest: we've looked at the "time" we believe rapture is most likely to occur, in the chronology of events: so let's continue.

1st Corinthians 15;50 declares ***"But now is Christ risen from the dead, and become the firstfruits of them that slept."*** In the fact that the word "first-fruit" is used, we know this is a term of planting, growing, and harvest. So, we turn to 1st Thessalonians 4;13-18 to find the "harvest" of them that sleep in Christ.

We find that to also be the very same Scripture we use to explain the "rapture" of all who are Born Again! And that gives us the first 2 parts, or phases, of this specific harvest! Leaving only one more phase; which is called "gleaning"! And gleaning is that part of harvest where whatever may have been dropped, or otherwise escaped the reaper, is picked up from the field.

In fact: in the Bible's lesson of harvest, it was a command from God that the corners of the fields be intentionally left un-harvested.

The purpose for this "gleaning" was that it could then be gathered by the poor; and those in need. But as we relate the message of this harvest to people; it leaves us with a problem. Because we've already said that rapture happens *before* Tribulation begins; that forces us to the conclusion that the gleaning phase must happen *during* Tribulation!

So: how does the Bible answer it all? And who are the people who will be taken in this gleaning?

In study, we find that the answer is found under the fifth seal of Revelation 6. Plus: we take note of the fact that this entire picture has been so important to God, that He's hidden all of it under this seal! In fact; the entire 5th seal is devoted to people who are "Martyred" for Christ's sake!

In Revelation 6;9; when "The Lamb of God" opens the 5th seal, a body of people are seen in heaven, "under the altar". Insight helps us understand that by being "under the altar", these people have qualified to be their own sacrifice! We must understand that none of them qualify to be a sacrifice for someone else. That fact is what separates Jesus from all others who are martyred. But because God gives them the distinction of being a martyr for Jesus Christ: offering themselves in Christ's name: that helps us see why they're important enough for God to hide them under the altar, and under one of the seals.

Specifically; because: this keeps Satan & Co. from having access to them. Which we will look at later on.

From the 9th through 11th verses of chapter 6; we find these people asking God to avenge their blood: crying out for vengeance and justice because they've been murdered on the earth. White robes are given them, and they're told to "rest yet for a time"; because there's another group of people who will join them.

This 2nd group will have been murdered and become martyrs as they are. But: The second group is "the gleaning"!

We find them again: (these people of the gleaning): in the 20th chapter of Revelation. Verse 4 is clear in the description of them: declaring ***"and I saw the souls of them that were beheaded for the witness of Jesus, and for the word of God, and which had not worshipped the beast, neither his image, neither had received his mark upon their foreheads, or in their hands"***.

That's the essence of being a martyr for Christ's sake! But as we've said, and as we're going to show; there's something else about these people: (who are the gleaning): but it's going to astonish some, and probably anger many others.

There's one word that will completely describe the resistance of these people, as it relates to their confrontation with "the mark of the beast". As we've said, that word is "overcome"!

And we see it used as an instruction to all 7 of the Churches found in t he 2nd and 3rd chapters of Revelation! That's what we've all been missing through the years! That's what's confused so many of us, as we've tried to apply this message to ourselves.

We know that Salvation comes to us only through our Faith in and confession of Jesus Christ. That our "inner being": which is our "individual and human spirit"; comes to life because we believe what we publicly say about Jesus. But, to Overcome is a work! It describes an action! It's a description of being able to gain victory over the "mark of the beast" through one's own efforts: even though that effort does result in the person being a sacrifice and a martyr! Because these people are so important to God that He's hidden them "under a seal", they're also important enough for Jesus to give them a message of instruction in how to overcome, and what things they will need to do in order to overcome. He even encourages them with special rewards: just one of which will be the glory of setting with Him as ruler on the earth, for a thousand years!

As we've studied the subject of "martyrdom" through the years; one special thing has become clear to us. That's in how God looks upon people who willingly give up their lives for a "just" cause. We see it in statements like "blessed is the man who gives up his life for a friend"; and others. Even though we can't know for certain which ones are Born Again, and which are not: it doesn't seem to matter so much; because it's obvious that God has a special place in His heart for warriors who die on the field of battle. And through the slaying of "the Lamb of God" and the sacrifice of Jesus Christ; surely God now knows the pain and suffering of this kind of service. In our own minds we elevate these martyrs in our esteem, and in our honor of them; believing that what they've done: (and what these people will do): is truly worthy of praise. But have we ever considered our lives of daily, living sacrifice? Have we ever thought it worthy of note to God? Can we see that in the mind of God, for us to spend a lifetime as a "follower of Jesus Christ" is worthy of the same kind of honor God gives a Martyr?

As a matter of fact; if we look for it, we can find an abundance of evidence to prove that the reward for the Born Again, is surely equal to ruling for a thousand years. All that's laid up in heaven; will be shared with these martyrs, because they're going to become a part of *our* group. Just because Jesus is focused upon them here; and is giving them encouragement to "Overcome the mark of the beast"; none of us should ever allow petty jealousy or envy of them to cloud the awesomeness of God's system of rewards.

Under the 5th Seal

We've tried to lay as much stress as we could on the fact that the Martyrs of God are hidden exclusively under the 5th seal. But there's so much more to see, we've decided to make the subject an entire chapter.

An overview of the 5th---8th chapters of Revelation shows us that the entirety of God's power to regain full and complete control of the earth; and to bring judgment upon it; is under these first 7 seals. The importance and value to God that these seals represent, is therefore far more than anyone has shown us to date. For instance: each one of these seals represents a special and particular power that's in the hands of "the Lamb of God"; whom we believe is also Jesus Christ and Messiah.

As we've said already, under the 5th seal we can find no other subject than that of the martyrs of God! That fact, and the importance of the seals obviously causes us to ask "why" and "what". Why is this subject so important to God? And what is there about martyrdom that has application to Tribulation and the End Time?

Within "the great commission" we teach, is "the Good News" of Salvation through Jesus Christ. We also teach that there's only "one way" to gain Salvation and have everlasting life with God. In fact; Jesus declared "no man cometh to the Father except by me"! And so; that "one way" is because of the sacrifice and suffering of Jesus: who, we believe and teach, took upon Himself the entirety of our individual burden of accountability, and "paid" for our sins through shedding His own blood and life for us. We declare that He would have done this, even if we: (each of us individually): were the only "unsaved" person to have ever lived upon the earth.

But then we run into these martyrs for Christ: people who have; and who will give up their lives because they stand as witness for Christ's sake! And we find that in God's eyes, to be a martyr is to become *ones own sacrifice*! And we become a bit confused; over the difference between "works" and "Grace" all over again. So, let's look at it straight on. Understanding will surely clarify:

Different from dieing a "natural death" or in war, or even in some form of accident: being a martyr for Christ's sake is to be **murdered** because one stands upon their testimony of Christ Jesus. And we find that God is so honored by this form of offering; and so willing to honor the one who sacrifices their life for Christ; He declares it worthy of special note.

Look back at the Scripture for example; and note that "white robes" are given these people under the altar. One of the few places where white robes are presented, is to "the Bride of Christ" as she's "made herself ready". Can we take that to mean that these people: (these martyrs): are a part of the Bride? Answer: *We'd better*; because everything we know about this first group declares that every one of them is ***Born Again***!!

Question: "Because the 5th seal only comes into existence with the systems called "Martyrdom"; "New Birth" and "Salvation"; is it possible that even we have a place under or within its power"? Answer: Absolutely! Because we also "testify" and "bear witness" of Jesus Christ, that's a part of belonging under the 5th seal, even though we aren't martyred, or even mentioned. Also note:

A robe is something one uses to cover a body: as in "body of flesh". It's tangible; made of substance; so the symbolism of white robes is something else we need to look at. Compare it to the covering God gave Adam and Eve as an example of where to start. However:

It just may be that these robes are made and given more to protect those who look upon the people qualified to wear them, than they are a covering over our naked body! For example: If the glorious living spirits of the people of the Bride of Christ is returned to it's place outside our body of flesh: as we've said it was before Adam sinned: wouldn't that bring on a need to have our flesh covered; so that natural people wouldn't be damaged by the strength of this glory? Also:

Among other things, God has taught us that to Him, a white robe is a sign, or a symbol of purity, cleanliness, and worthiness. When God gives someone a white robe, it's a sign or signal that no matter what they may think of themselves; God is giving them "credit" for being all the things Jesus has accomplished, even though we've done nothing more than to believe on Jesus and confess His glory. Being given "credit" for worthiness that we know we've done almost nothing to earn, is probably our greatest "hang-up" in being a Christian.

In a sense, it seems we have a justifiable argument against receiving this greatness: we're uncomfortable with the picture of it: and if it wasn't for the fact that these honors are also a part of our Salvation, we'd probably reject them entirely. But, if we turn it all around, and look at this through God's eyes: the first thing we'd see is the insult that just a hint of rejection brings against the honors that have been so "hard gained" by Christ Jesus. We'd see that from God's point of view, we give far greater honor and praise to Christ, by freely, willingly, knowingly accepting these honors and credit for accomplishment. When we stand with Christ in righteousness, while we're being given credit for having perfect justification; that's a true mark of our understanding!

When we can declare ourselves to be "sons of God", at the same time that God declares us to "be His sons"; we honor God's intent and desire to build an everlasting kingdom; filled with people who have all the qualifications of Jesus Christ. As was said many years ago; "God is so proud of that boy of His, He's going to make a bunch of people who look and act just like Him"!!

The essence of the message to the people of the 7 Churches is that IF they will "overcome", God will give them a place in His eternal and everlasting kingdom.

We have to deal with the situation though, in order to get out of their way! And some are going to resist to the very end.

We use several references to teach one another that no one can gain Salvation through "works": and Ephesians 2; 8 & 9 says it as well as any: ***"For by grace are ye saved through faith; and that not of yourselves: it is the gift of God: Not of words, lest any man should boast".*** And yet!!

As we've said: If we look back in "secular" history: (the Roman Empire for example): we'll find what happened to the first group that caused them to become martyrs. It also just "jumps out" at us, that these people were also Born Again before they were martyred! That adds a bit to our confusion; because we know the 2nd group: (which will also be murdered and join the first group): are not Born Again before Tribulation begins. They couldn't be, because if they were Born Again they would go with us in the rapture---provided it does come before Tribulation.

That fact changes the entire picture of the 1st and 2nd group of martyrs. But we need to set down some other information before we can look at how they're united into one group.

The 2nd group of martyrs can only come into existence after the beginning of the Great Tribulation. That's shown in Revelation 6;11. In this verse the 1st group is told to ***"rest yet for a little season, until*** *their fellow-servants also and their brethren, that should be killed as they were, should be fulfilled"*. Also keep in mind that these "fellow-servants---and their brethren": (the 2ⁿᵈ group): are the gleaning phase of Christ's harvest of the people who "sleep in Christ" plus those "who are alive and remain". This is the entire body of people who are Born Again? However:

With Jesus Christ being the "first-fruits" of them that sleep; and our "rapture" being the second phase of this entire harvest: that means following the rapture there will be **no one** left upon the earth who is Born Again.

Even these people who are the gleaning will go into the Great Tribulation being "unsaved". Because they've obviously rejected Christ Jesus; else they would have gone with the rest of us at rapture.

After the rapture; things change! We see part of that change in Revelation 14;6 where an angel of God flies *"in the midst of heaven"*, preaching what's called "the everlasting gospel; which is *"Fear God, and give glory to him; for the hour of his judgment is come: and worship him that made heaven, and earth, and the sea, and the fountains of waters"*. The message from Jesus Christ, given in the 2ⁿᵈ and 3ʳᵈ chapters of Revelation, becomes the most important words that the people of the gleaning can hear!

Because it's a message of "overcoming" and finding a "victory" *only* through becoming a martyr! It's the message that results in part of what's said in the 4ᵗʰ verse of Revelation 20:

"And I saw the souls of them that were beheaded for the witness of Jesus, and for the word of God, and which had not worshipped the beast: neither his image, neither had received his mark upon their foreheads, or in their hands; and they lived and reigned with Christ a thousand years". Again! These are the **gleaning**! But they must gain their everlasting life through becoming "their own sacrifice"! God is able to give them a place in His eternal kingdom through their *specific work* of becoming a martyr. But *only* through this *one specific act---not* a "body of works"! But please note this:

Because it's possible to gain a place in eternity through becoming a martyr: specifically, through *dieing* and being *transformed back* to life everlasting, it was also terribly important that this knowledge be held in *secret*. That's why God had to put it all under one of the Seals! But it doesn't stop there.

When the beast of Revelation 13 does find out that it's possible to gain everlasting physical life through this process of dieing and being transformed back to life; **that** becomes the power through which he returns "life" to one of his 7 heads: which is the man we call "the man of sin"; "the son of perdition"; and the "human form of the spirit of anti-Christ"!! We might even suggest that instead of this "head" being an honored part of the beast, he's little more than **an experiment**! But please take note:

This is "the mark of the beast"! This is everlasting life apart from God! This is why it's such a blasphemy before God, because people who take this mark will live forever in their body of flesh! But, only we seem to know that their eternity will be in "the Lake of Fire"!

This mark of the beast is the falseness of real Salvation which is still now offered through the real Jesus Christ. It's been said many times; that before one can copy and falsify, there must already exist the true and the original!

This is what this false Christ will offer as "credentials"; to try to prove that he is Christ. This may very well be the "strong delusion" that comes upon the people who take this mark: that they believe the lie of it.

In Romans 10; 9&10, the words are as clear as any can make them: *"That if thou shalt confess with thy mouth the Lord Jesus, and shalt believe in thine heart that God hath raised Him from the dead, thou shalt be saved". "For with the heart man believeth unto righteousness; and with the mouth confession is made unto salvation".* This is how we pass from being "unsaved" to being "saved".

Through this public confession and belief, the Spirit of God is able to enter into our being and bring "life" to our dead spirit! And then; through passing from life; to death; to life again; we're promised to be given a New and everlasting body of flesh, that will not only "look like" the body Jesus showed after resurrection; but which will operate like His: (appearing in closed rooms and such). So basically: is that so much different from what these martyrs are promised? Even though the martyr goes almost immediately to the place where they're to be murdered for bearing witness of Jesus, is it all that different from living our a life of stress and satanic attack because we live our lives in witness of Jesus Christ? The point we're leading up to is this: Although we have 2 ways of gaining the primary promise: (one through confession and Faith: two through confession and death): after that the martyr is given a "living spirit"; a new and everlasting body of flesh: and everlasting life with God. That are numbered in company with the entire harvest---which isn't complete until all 3 phases of it are finished!

Once more, we remind ourselves that it's God's real and true intent that NONE should perish. So, maybe we haven't even seen all of His provisions for getting as many as He can! And maybe our difference of opinion over what God is going to do is just personal.

Our Personal Relationship

In Revelation 1; verses 13 to 16, John describes Jesus Christ as He is today! Different in appearance from the man who walked the earth: different even from the Son of God who arose from the grave: this is Jesus as "the Lion of the tribe of Judah! Messiah to the house of Israel! King above all kings!

From our lesson, we know that flesh and blood: (in combination): cannot inherit the kingdom of God. We've done the research and come to the conclusion that it's the infusing power of Holy Ghost that now causes the great change in Jesus, from what he looked like when He ascended from the earth. His hair is now as white as snow! Denoting great wisdom! His eyes are as a flame of fire: piercing through to the truth of any and all: although we still don't know what color they are! His skin color is described as being the color of hot brass, glowing as though it's just been taken from the furnace! And His entire appearance is more radiant than is the sun at noon-day. And because we're told that we'll see Him as He is, because our appearance will be "like His"; we have all the evidence we need to support the mind picture of **us** looking nearly the same as Jesus looks. Including the "aura" of the Spirit emanating from within us! To us; that means there's going to be a greater change in us than even in what we see in Jesus. We have farther to go in the first place---coming from where we are right now. Plus; and still for us, the change to our entire being is also going to be tremendous; because we haven't moved all that far from what we were the day we were Born Again. One of the better ways of describing the changes within us; is that we're going to go from "seeing" with the eyes of man, to seeing with the eyes of God. Actually; that's something we *should* be trying to do right now; but the flesh *is* strong.

In all the lessons we have, we have nothing to suggest we won't become "the Bride of Christ". But: We're still "the Body of Christ" at this time!

In the book of Genesis, Eve is described as being a "help-meet": not a help-mate. The difference in those 2 words, is that one who is a help-***meet***, is not only worthy of the position; but actually knows what's required to fill

34

it. Just that, should be enough for us to understand that in the eternity to come: and as a collective unit: we will hold both positions: Body of Christ; and Bride of Christ! And be a help-***meet*** in both of them. That shows us we're also going to go through another tremendous change; because there will be absolutely no schism in our relationship with Christ---nor in our relationships with one another. There will be no position greater or lesser than any other! No one individual will hold a unity with Christ stronger than any other! No inner group: (or clique): working for greater benefit or advantage than others have will be allowed. Simply because there will be no need or desire for it.

All these changes, which are contrary to the basic nature of mankind, surely must come upon us different from what we now all seem to assume.

Because today; if anyone talks about it at all, it seems that everyone just assumes we're going to be suddenly changed into this "New creature", with all knowledge; all wisdom: and all love. Certainly! All sin is going to be removed from us! That's going to be a relief we can't even begin to imagine right now. But the one thing God is never going to remove from us is the authority and power of choice. And in choice is the authority to accept or reject. Therefore all these things that God wants us to become, must be shown to us. We have to be given all the knowledge about every one of them in order to choose.

That's one of the reasons we have so much "trouble" today in making choices: because Satan & Co. are always trying to manipulate our information. They try to turn and twist our information and knowledge so that our choices give them an advantage.

God doesn't work that way now! Neither will He change in the eternal future!

We're each one as individually different from one another as are individual flakes of snow! And because God shows us He truly enjoys diversity and difference; we've no reason to believe He's going to change us so much we end up looking all the same. So, like the stranger looking at a flock of sheep and seeing none of the individuals; while the shepherd sees every individual animal: as we're seen from the outside; and by people who don't belong to our group, the millions and millions of us seem to be just a mass of people. But because the Bible declares we'll be known as we were known, we'll obviously know more about the people we've had close relationships with on the earth. But can we imagine, in the Body, never meeting a stranger? Never distrusting or fearing that person before we come to know them? That's just a part of our eternity; and sometimes it's really hard to contain the absolute wonder and joy that's the promise of our eternal life!

Every human is born as; and we live our earthly lives as a single solitary individual. In our aloneness and individuality, we maintain a control over the relationships we have. Pushing some away, while we try to draw others closer. But God is different in His relationships---which shouldn't surprise even one of us.

When God comes into a relationship, all of Him comes. He doesn't hold anything back, or keep things in reserve. Because there's so much of God though, we seem to always be running into new and different things about Him. Things we've never seen, or things we couldn't understand until we grew and developed enough to understand them. For example:

Have we reached the strength of spiritual development enough to understand that God is so complex in what He is, that He can have an individual relationship with literally millions of people all at the same time? Or are we still locked into childishness and immaturity so strong that it keeps from even trying to understand this awesome ability of God?

Can we understand that God is so strong in His ability to control His own mind, that He can actually and literally remove things from His mind, and never remember them again? How well we understand that is a measure of how well we actually trust God! And how well we believe our sins are truly forgiven! Because God has said He would "remember them no more"! By the way: that's another of our "hang-ups"; over confessed sin. It's also compounded by the fact that we can't forgive ourselves of our sins; and because other Christians won't forgive us of them either.

In the chapter titled "The Body of Christ", we've looked at the fact that sin restricts our mind capacity somewhere between 75 and 90 percent. And we also looked at some of the possibilities, when our entire existence is free from sin and Satan.

With the restriction removed from our minds, isn't it likely that we'll also rid ourselves of many of these immature and childish Hang-ups? For example.

Mental maturity: of the kind we're talking about; will remove childish jealousy: tantrums of want and desire: and the ego that claims the world resolves around "me. But we can also see a potential problem, which must be dealt with: because:

Even though all the restrictions are removed from our minds; our individual power of **choice** will never be taken away! And that leads to the conclusion that sin absolutely must be removed from creation! Because even the increased intellect of some people would only show them how to sin with even greater strength, if it remained in existence.

Two Pictures---One Person

Under God's plan, Jesus Christ has been "given" to the Gentiles: (us): because it's the only way we could be brought into God's everlasting Kingdom: and because the nation of Israel will only accept Messiah!

In His ability to know what the future holds, God knew this would happen. That's where, and why, we get the two pictures of Jesus. One, is of Jesus as the "King above all kings: "the Lion of the tribe of Judah": and Messiah to the house of Israel. And the second picture is what's called "the suffering Messiah" who we come to believe in, and hold in such great esteem; because Jesus Christ has chosen to go to Calvary for our sakes.

Through study; we've come to the conclusion that because the nation of Israel is "chosen by God" and God has made covenant with them through their fathers: (Abraham; Isaac; and Jacob): God's intent for this entire "blood line" of people is that they all will be resurrected! See Romans 11;26-28 and Ezekiel 37.

Our studies have also shown us that because Israel is to be given a "terrestrial" body of flesh: (see Romans 15; 35-46): God's intent for them is to also take up the position Adam was given: (Dominion): before he sinned; but that will be on the "new earth" God will make after this one is destroyed.

From out of that same Scripture though: (Romans 15; 35-46): we're shown that our "new bodies of flesh" are called "celestial": which is more of a designation than an actual difference; because their terrestrial bodies obviously won't be imprisoned on the earth; and to this dimension; the way ours are. We do see what is most probably the major difference between their bodies and ours though. Because study of "the body of Christ": (us): shows that we're going to eventually be *fixed* in the numbers of people who will be members of it. God knows!! But once those who are Born Again are combined with those who will be "martyred" for Christ's sake, that number will be established and finished. No more will be added.

While the people of the house of Israel are shown to have bodies that will have the capacity to repopulate the new earth. And it will need to be repopulated: because by the end of the Great Tribulation, we're told that the death rate will have been so great that there will only be several million people left, instead of the billions that are now alive. There's also some evidence that supports the claim that there will be Gentile people: (non Jew): who survive into and through the millennium at least. Look at Revelation 20; 8-10. However; with the last half of the Great Tribulation being shown as "either/or": (either take the "mark of the Beast" or be beheaded): this is the only Scripture we can find to support this claim.

After the thousand years are finished; and this promise to the house of Israel is complete; the Bible is silent on the subject of what will Jesus be doing after that. We know that one of the promises from God is that the throne of David will never set empty. In fact; and take note: ***someone*** is setting on it right now! And how many kings or queens can we count today? But because **King David** is among those who are resurrected into everlasting life; we've formed the opinion that he will return to that post. But that's also "God's business". The point we're working to show, is that because we will be who and what we are; wherever Jesus goes, and whatever He's involved in doing, we'll be there---helping Him do whatever it is; always!

Another thing we've concluded about our eternal future is that the lifetime we spend upon this earth, and the stress and pressures we deal with, are a "training ground", or "boot camp" for what God intends for us after this life

Jesus Christ---the "head" of our body---is like us, in that He **also** has known all the stress and temptations we've known. So; if these things are for future and eternal use, we can begin to form ideas of what we'll be doing.

Most of what we come up with is likely to be "just speculation" and "day dreaming"; but when we take sin out of our picture, as the saying goes "the sky's the limit" on what things we can imagine. One thing we can be sure of is that the time between today and the day of "the end" is going to continue to be filled with events of stress, conflict, struggle, and frustration. Although we may not directly participate, we're going to witness events, and the workings of beings we don't have the mental capacity to even imagine right now.

We're likely to be "flooded" with things too great and too complicated to control; and only our anchor in Jesus Christ, and one another, will keep us from loosing our mind altogether! So it's now become "vital" that we study the truth! That we learn; through developing a relationship with Holy Ghost and with Christ Jesus!

Israel demands a king! And although they did it before; and ended up in a "mess": this time Israel is so determined to have the king that's promised in prophecy, they've rejected any and all who said, or say, they're Israel's king. They rejected Jesus, because they wanted "the Lion of the tribe of Judah", and God gave them "the suffering Messiah", Jesus Christ. They're paying the penalty for that right now; along with some other penalties God has been forced to allow them to suffer through. But one day the penalties will be over! The time of suffering will be ended for them! And Israel will know a short time of peace: which sadly will all come crashing down when they see "the Abomination of Desolation" standing in Jerusalem.

But! Prophecy will be fulfilled! Israel will get her King! And He will be "the Lion of the tribe of Judah"! But He will also be Jesus Christ!

And when they find out who He is: and that they could have had Him 2,000 years ago; they're going to set up a wailing over Him that will surely make the rest of us sad for their sakes. But there's another part of the prophecy that gives us an insight into the 1,000 years of this reign of Christ. The part that says *"rule with a rod of iron"*!

And although we don't think of this as being a literal iron rod; the "rule of Law" which Messiah will use during this time; is comparable with the unyielding and unbending nature of iron. In one place for example; it's said that if a person doesn't come to Jerusalem once a year to worship, the penalty will be that it won't rain on that person's crop the following year.

The part that simply "blows our minds", is that even with the real and true Messiah Jesus Christ setting in Jerusalem; some people will be so obstinate they will refuse to worship Him. That's got to be the height of stupid! But if there was going to be no people who refuse to worship; there would have been no need to tell us about it.

But this is a public picture of Jesus the world will see. In the privacy of our union with Him, we're going to experience something else.

This is our Jesus: "our friend and brother"; and in this case Husband to our collective Bride. He's the person whose strength of love for us is so strong in Him that He truly wants to spend eternity with us.

Our knowledge of Jesus allows us to blend the 2 pictures together, and see only one person. Our individual relationship with Him is likely to continue the way it's started---with Jesus having the ability to be with each one of us as though we were the only person alive.

We simply don't have the mental capacity to explain how it's possible for Him to do this; but He does! The only thing any of us needs to know is that "it is what it is"; and we can glory in it.

To have a personal; private; even an intimate relationship with Jesus Christ; that comes through Holy Ghost, our constant Comforter: is surely something every Christian wants to improve and stabilize in their lives. And it seems like it should be something we shouldn't have to work all that hard to have: especially when all the parties involved want the same thing. But our enemy stands at everyone's gate; and wants nothing more than to wreck all the good things we could have. But:

There's a kind of spirit moving about the world that causes everyone to sense that the end isn't far off. We see the results of it in our lack of patience: in our harshness of relationships with others: in what's being called "road rage": going Postal: and many other things like these. But the comfort and message from God says "I never said it would be easy: I only said it would be worth it".

When we allow Comforter to "touch" our emotions; as we look upon the 2 pictures of Christ; feelings within us seem to build without restriction. And suddenly our entire being is overwhelmed and shaking with Love and Pride of Jesus: with Glory, as His Victory comes upon us: and with a Joy unspeakable; because within and behind the Glory of Christ is our personal relationship with Him. How can it get any better than that??

The Body of Christ

As we were explaining the unity of "the body of Christ" a few years ago: and the fact that this body is primarily "*female dominant*" in its character and personality: it suddenly came into our mind that one of our good friends was trying to picture an actual and literal woman in his mind. We found out later, that his thought was of some gigantic female body, with Jesus Christ somehow setting on top of it: He'd even complicated that, by trying to mentally picture himself somehow being transformed and changed, so he would have a female body.

We've told this story a few times, as a way of showing how literal some people are, when their focus on things physical dominates their thinking. So even though it may take some time to get it all straight in our head; let's enjoy the study anyway. Because: not only is *our place*, in the body of Christ, everlasting; it's also one of the most Glorious positions God sets us into. And there's tremendous reward in understanding what God is doing with this great unit of people.

The Body of Jesus Christ is a totally real "body of people"! And there *is* a way to make a comparison of the entirety to the way human beings are mostly dominated by physical thoughts and attitude. If a person is a female and a woman, they're mostly dominated by personality, character, thoughts and attitude that are female in nature: and just the opposite is true if they're a male. His thoughts; his attitude, personality and character are mostly male in nature. That's what we mean as we say that the Body of Christ is "female dominant"! As a collective unit; our dominant thoughts, personality, character and attitude is mostly female in nature. Men are not going to have to worry about God changing them into a woman.

Neither should women begin to think that God is going to change things and allow women to become as dominating as men have been: our way of using *that* has been wrong, wrong for thousands of years anyway! However; and basically; as Paul explains it in Galatians 3;26&27; *"there is neither male nor female: for ye are all one in Christ Jesus"*. In any definition or description of uniting male *with* female; the essence of the definition is that both sides are equal: neither being greater or lesser than the other. Plus, in the joining of male *to* female: (like marriage is supposed to be): we add one and one, and end up with one. And if we don't understand that; maybe we should rethink how prepared we are for marriage.

For many Christians; this entire picture is another of those, so called, "burdens of Salvation" people think about. Because even though we understand that the Body of Christ is a very large body of people: probably numbering in the hundreds of millions: when God tells us we're given the position of standing with Christ Jesus in this Kingdom; in equality and as Joint Heirs with Him, we only "see" with human eyes, instead of God's eyes.

And human thinking says man can *never* be equal with Jesus, no matter how many of us there are.

Certainly: Romans 12;3 does tell us that a Christian is "***not to think of himself more highly than he ought to think***": but if we'll study that, we'll see it's in reference to comparing ourselves with one another.

The "bottom line" is that we're getting close to insult against God: or at least showing our ignorance: if we don't try to think as highly of our "collective unit" as God does. **And**: of the people who add together to make it up. And God loves us so much He sent Jesus Christ to sacrifice Himself for us!

God just astonishes us, by giving us "credit" for doing many of the things Jesus did: even though we know we aren't even worthy to qualify for doing them. But this is "God's way", even if we privately try to disagree with it. That's where a problem begins.

Romans 14; 12-14 shows us that God has set Himself in the position of "judging us"---the Body of Christ. And if we then judge one another: (in ignorance or intent): basically we're telling God we don't believe He qualifies to do that work. That's scary!! It's also something the devil would like us to keep on doing; because it's a cause for schism in the Body--- something else God doesn't like! And truly; if we even privately disagree with God over the qualifications He says He's given to everyone alike; or the works He "credits" us with having done; that's also judging, and not allowing God to do His job.

The conclusion is; that it's wrong for us to praise, worship and glorify our God, for doing all the awesome things He's done; and then turn around and say we aren't worthy to accept them, and can't believe they were done for our sakes! That's hypocrisy!

There's an "old adage" that says "familiarity breeds contempt". Basically it means that the more familiar and adjusted we are to something, the less we continue to give it honor and esteem. Familiarity with our Salvation comes when people start thinking it's easily gained, or it's without cost or hardship.

In some people, we've even seen that Born Again has deteriorated to the point of being little more than the password or "key to the club" we all belong to. The simple fact is that if we don't honor something we have, how can we expect others to honor it?

If we don't honor the things God has given us; or the positions He's placed us in: (which is something we do when we disagree with God by saying we aren't worthy to hold these things): that's a   dishonor of them that does border on insult.

As a class of people: (Gentile): God has done us a great honor by "giving" us Jesus Christ; so that we could have everlasting life and positive relationship with Him! And the Bible leaves no doubt but that we have almost nothing to compare it with.

As humans; in all of the things and beings God could have chosen to have personal and individual relationship with; He's set us at the top of that list. In fact we're the **only** beings formed "in the image of God". We have no evidence that angels are 3 part beings. In fact, what we see inclines us to think they're more likely 2 part beings. In this, Satan is the example; and it's clear that he doesn't understand the 3rd part: (spirit): of humans.

In essence, God has said that out of all the creatures and beings His limitless imagination could have created; He's chosen the form of human being to "look like". And throughout the endless future, the structure and form of human being: (2 arms, 2 legs, 1 head): is what God obviously sees as the better way to enjoy that future.

But first; we have to step into the area of "mind pictures" or "imagination" to see the possibilities of "what will be" in that future. Oh, we can wait until that future becomes a reality; but only a few of us are satisfied to do that. So we have a "first problem": (and it's an entertaining problem instead of being a hardship): but it will be how to work in and explore the possibilities of an entire creation that's totally absent of sin.

In other words, we want to examine as much of eternity as we can, after sin, and after the entire company we call Satan & Co. are forever removed. Sure! The Bible says we can't "picture" things to come with our imagination. But that's not an excuse to "do nothing" people use it for. Because the very next verse tells us that the Spirit of God will and can show us these things.

We've never had this kind of experience before; so many of the things we want to work with the Spirit and see, immediately begins to stretch the limits of our minds ability.

By the way; the limits of our mind is something else we're going to have to learn to live with, after sin is gone. Because: and as we've said: Scientists don't all agree on a number; so they tell us that humans only use between 10% and 25% of the total capacity of our brain. And that something restricts us from using or even developing the rest of that capacity. We, who are Christian; and followers after Jesus Christ can immediately tell them what that restriction is. It's sin!

So, with sin and Satan removed, the mind restriction we now have to live with should also be gone. Have we given that any consideration. Can we even picture ourselves being 75 to 90 times smarter than we are? Can we even think of what areas of our mind will be opened up? But that's only among the first things that awaits in our future; and will surely happen almost immediately after we get our "New Body". So, maybe it will be possible for us to know and be able to understand far more than we do now. But it won't actually be because we'll get a New Body of flesh. It will be because we've escaped the restriction of sin upon our brain. Please note:

Although we don't know a lot about Adam and Eve before they sinned: what we do have shows that when they sinned, not only did that stop their face to face relationship with God; it must have also stopped all of their non-physical insights and abilities as well. That leads us to believe that when the restriction on our brain is removed, so too will be our restriction against seeing into these now invisible worlds around us. Even now we have some small ability in that area: calling it a 6th sense, ESP; or a "medium"; and others.

But we shouldn't take the possibilities of having an unrestricted mind too far. Look what Adam and Eve did with theirs!

Another thing we've found to be "God's way": different from "man's way": is in how He operates His "reward system".

When God uses someone, without first asking them to choose to participate; God is so powerful it almost looks like He's forcing them to join in. In a fashion that's probably true. But when humans do it, it's usually without any kind of reward, whether the work is a success or not. But with God, the reward he lays on people afterward, is almost always *greater* than would have been His reward if they had been allowed to choose. For instance:

God has chosen to hide and protect women in a 2nd class position: which is clearly a tremendous burden on them. But we can be totally sure that what He's done, will accomplish a part of His plan that leads to complete and total Victory over all of God's enemies. Through Eve, God even allowed us all to make a mistake, that's kept all women in and under a cloud: because under Law, it's almost a violation; and clearly unfair to force all women to share Eve's penalty! Eve was the only one to eat of that fruit! So we have to ask "why force all women to suffer for her mistake?

None of us knows the entirety of what the burden upon women is: or what more it's designed to accomplish. There's one thing all woman can take encouragement from: That as it was when Jesus asked God if there wasn't "some other way"? God's silence was His answer. And in this work and plan of God, no matter how frustrating it gets, God's answer to women is still, "there just wasn't any other way"!

From the sin of Eve until this very hour, to be born female is to be required to participate in the ongoing burden that Eve's mistake has laid upon all women. Not one has been asked to willingly participate; although the obvious importance of this is so clear that if asked, most women would likely agree to join in. Most agree that it would really be "nice" if they were asked though. But since they aren't, we have reason to expect God's reward to every woman will be even greater than it would have been if they had been asked.

We know that human marriage is intended to be a living example of what our relationship between Jesus Christ and the Body of Christ is going to be. Of course we first have to take out the mistakes; the abuses; and the problems that come from lack of knowledge.

Then, we have to remind the men in the Body of Christ, that no matter what position of leadership God has put them in, He **never** took them out of the Body and put them in the head!

And *then*; we need to tell the men that only if they treat their wives the same way Jesus treats the Body of Christ, do they then qualify to be "head" over her!

As the title of this study suggests, once we come to find and then understand these things of **truth**, then we can feel the security and inner peace that's a part of their design. This is also a part of the "power of knowledge": which is actually greater than is the power of great wealth.

As things are beginning to "heat up" and the pressures in the world increase; now is not the time to "fall away" or turn back to our old ways either.

Contrary to what appears to be the general attitude; of just waiting for Jesus to "come and get us"; the longer we wait here on earth, the more apparent it should become that God is "waiting on us" to do something for Him still! When we find what that "something" is and do it: (and it's given in this study): only then will we have a proper right to wait for the Lord.

It's terribly hard; if not impossible, to draw a mental image of the size of the Body of Christ. After all it's been building for the past 2,000 years, and most of its members are "asleep in Christ" already. In fact, the great number of people who make up this Body actually leads to one of our greater mistakes. That mistake is our effort to be "separatists" or to isolate one group from another. But it's leading us into one of the better "rules of war", which is "divide and conquer". So: lets look at this "head on", so we can at least be aware that what so many might think is a good thing, has been turned against us.

If we'd just look back, at the history of denominational separation, it's likely we'd all agree that the concept of separating denominations is quite possibly one of the greater disasters Satan & Co. have forced us into. Because one of the greater wrongs denominational thinking does at the very beginning, is to separate us from being a collective unit.

It took God a long time to teach us why; and for what purpose He even tolerated denominations. So as we share that lesson, please be aware that although it's easy enough to understand; we still have a lot of problems with it: which is certainly a reflection *against us*, and not against God.

As it began, the "problem" we had was in our inability to understand how 2 or 3 people could read the same passage or verse of Scripture, and gain 3 different "interpretations" of what it said. And surely, that gets terribly complicated when millions of people all seem to each have a different idea. God explained it this way:

As we've said, God enjoys diversity! He likes individual distinctions, because they're a mark of freedom and choice. In fact, there are no 2 things that have come from the creative hand of God which are exactly the same. Not even twins! There's also so much to do already in God's kingdom that almost nothing would be accomplished if we were all doing the same thing. It's more complicated than what we're showing, but we are trying to keep it simple.

What we do in life is motivated by what we ***believe***! And so; because God doesn't want us all doing the same thing, He actually encourages us to believe different things. In other words; change the belief, change what the believer does. And that's so simple, we had to wonder why we didn't think of it. However!

There are some things God simply will not compromise. In fact, neither does He encourage us to even have a differing opinion on them; because these things are "**fixed in stone**"!

To become a member of this "Body of Christ", every one of us must be Born Again! No ifs, ands, or buts. That means every one of us must also believe the 4 basic facts about Jesus Christ!

1. That Jesus is the **only** begotten Son of God
2. That Jesus was born from out of the body of a "**virgin**" woman
3. That Jesus sacrificed Himself in our place: **paying** our "sin penalty"
4. That Jesus **arose** from the grave of death and hell: and is now the Eternally Alive Son of God, seated at the honored right hand of the Father!

If we reject or compromise any one of these 4 specific things: no matter how they're worded: we ***have not*** received Salvation and we ***are not*** Born Again! But if we do believe and confess these things, not only are we Born Again, we're also named and counted as a member of the Body of Christ.

Please take note again:

There is nothing in this about Church membership; denominational thinking; or specific belief system. These things have no impact or influence upon us having or holding membership in the Body! In fact: As we can learn, God is very tolerant of our emotional debates and fierce rejections of one another's point of view or belief system.

Once we're truly Born Again, God gives us a great deal of freedom, in allowing us to choose what to believe; and the body of evidence we use to gain that conclusion. He warns us: that every man shall give account: (report): for what we've chosen to believe. And, He makes it clear that as He examines our report and reasons, no one else will be allowed to stand with us. We will each be judged individually! We will not be allowed to "blame" another; or use on another as an excuse for what we've chosen to believe either.

God's tolerance of what things we choose to believe right now, is also the beginning of a truly awesome insight into something else God is going to use throughout eternity! It's also a part of the way things will be after sin and Satan & Co. are forever removed from us. It's something we've been calling "the living environment of Grace"!

We know the word "Grace" means "un-merited favor". We've also found that after sin is gone, there's absolutely no limit to God's favor! He fully intends to pour it out on each one of us the same as He will pour it out on Jesus Christ! Without measure or limit! Knowing that is why we've spent time, trying to adjust ourselves to the magnificent generosity of God; as He credits us with things we haven't actually done; and gives us positions we believe we aren't qualified to fill.

When sin is forever gone from us, never again can anything we do be classified as sin! Things may be wrong, as we work to learn some process or action: And we know that as long as there's any process of learning new or different things, there will be mistakes! But those won't be sin! In this living environment of Grace, no one will ever sin by making a mistake! First because we won't be contaminated by sin: and Second because our mind will be changed to conform to the ways of God. Just the intellect and mind ability we're going to need in this environment of Grace will require all the improvement our new and unrestricted mind can supply. And even that won't be enough because we're still going to need the aid of God, through Holy Ghost!

Obviously the potentials and possibilities of this kind of life can never be completely explained with the mind power man has today! That's why the Bible speaks about "the imagination of our heart": not because the information isn't available, or that God is withholding it. It's because man; at this day and hour; just can't comprehend it all. But just to consider living in a world without sin: in a place where never again will anyone have to look over their shoulder to see who's watching: who's judging: is a mind freedom that touches us like a breath of fresh air.

We're also going to have to "break away" from a couple of specific things before we begin to understand even a small part of "the living environment of Grace". Because; and as we just mentioned: unless we can bring ourselves to work with the Spirit, and move beyond denominational thinking, or loyalty to a specific belief system; the freedom from restriction that's available to the Body of Christ is going to be terribly hard to gain.

Certainly! There is assurance and stability in holding on to habitual but non-advancing beliefs. That's why it's so hard to let go of them. But as is said in Hebrews 6;1&2: we're going to find denominational thinking and loyalty to a belief system are a part of the basic "principals of the doctrine of Christ.

And as we're given a list of what these principals are, we're also being told to "leave them": to "go on unto perfection". In fact; and as the writer of Hebrews makes plain; even our debates and worries over the stability and everlasting power of our Salvation is a part of this basic and foundational material.

Part of the reason we have "trouble" understanding and settling the issue of the Body of Christ, and the Bride of Christ; is that both are everlasting! That means there's less tolerance for mistake or personal idea as we study to find the fullness of them. There's even a kind of irony involved; (in Hebrews 6;4): because all of this has come from the awesomeness of the mind of God: and yet; even with our restricted minds, we've been in examination and judgment over what they are; and what they mean. Obviously, we've forgotten that the Bible warns against this: saying; the clay does not speak to the potter and tell them what to do!

From out of all the different groups of people we could set before us, and ask "is it possible that these are "The Bride of Christ"? Only those who are Born Again seem to stand up to the requirements and demands. Because those who are born again also meet the requirements for being "the Body of Christ" however; that *doesn't* exclude us from also being "the Bride" as well.

As we said earlier: it's hypocrisy for any of us to believe we're now a member of the Body of Christ, and then declare we aren't worthy, or aren't good enough to be members of either group. But! Please; **do** take note of this one!

When we take "the bread of Communion"; we're told that it's the symbol of "the broken body of Christ". However; no one has been teaching us that the word "broken" also means "divided" and "portioned out"! Therefore, no one has been teaching us that when we take this symbol into ourselves, it's also a sign of our willingness to be counted in the entire Body of Christ----which is "broken" and "portioned out" for us.

When we see this: that we're each being given an equal portion of the entire Body: this is absolutely the first step into understanding God's meaning and intent for communion. The peace and harmony we will feel toward all the other members of the Body; after we learn what we're doing by receiving "our part and portion"; is also something none of us has experienced before---simply because we didn't know! And the security we're going to know, through understanding just this part of the Body of Christ, is an ease and peace of mind that's beyond explaining!

The more things God opens up for our understanding and use; the more we find ourselves in astonishment and awe of God's mind and mental ability. Saying we're "stunned into silence" is a way to describe how it does touch us.

The Bride of Christ

Apart from the book of Revelation, the Bride of Jesus Christ isn't specifically shown anywhere else in the Bible. The reason we don't see her, is because she has no place or position in any world contaminated by sin! Certainly! All the "pieces" now exist. All the people who will belong to this great body of people are probably already alive: even though all of them may not be Born Again yet. All of the earthly things, which are part of the "make up" of the Bride come out of corruption; and therefore have to be transformed before they're placed within the Body. But, in order for us to gain some kind of insight into what the Bride of Christ is going to become: (or what she'll even look like): we need to understand this one thing about her.

The Bride of Christ, is God's "*reward*" to Jesus for all His work of sacrifice and substitution He's accomplished!! And if we'll consider everything we believe Jesus is worthy of receiving for that work: then add that the Bride is going to be equal to and worthy of being that reward: that will give us at least some idea of just how glorious God is going to make Her!

There are a couple of different opinions about whether or not God is going to *display* the Bride, to the world, before the Great Tribulation begins. Surely we can see the position of those who believe that the glory of the Bride will be such that the evil of this world couldn't even---shouldn't even---look upon her. And now that we see her as the specific reward for Christ Jesus that she is; no matter how proud of this Body we may be; maybe it would be better for us to give up any idea of an early earthly display.

Just the idea of the evil of this world looking upon such glory is close to being a disgusting "stomach turner": and everything we know says we're going to come to earth with Jesus; at "the second coming" anyway; so that should be display enough!!

Turning to more practical matters: We've said that both the Body of Christ; and the Bride of Christ are "female dominant in character, personality and nature. In other words; and even though there will be many men in this company: as a collective unit, we're going to not only think, but also act "female". And we quickly point out that as a woman, this Body and Bride is obviously far more---far greater than is any singular or human woman.

Normally, a great body of humans is similar to a flock of sheep without a shepherd: which is surely why God calls us sheep. And, by the way: many think of the cuddly little lamb as they think about God calling us sheep. But He says "sheep"; and there's nothing dumber on 4 legs. It's only as individuals and in small groups where we find the really intelligent human beings. But we do have reason to believe that with the sin restrictions removed, the intelligence level of either of these bodies will be far greater than the greatest genius now among us!

Comparing us to Eve: (the bride of Adam): the Bride of Christ is going to end up being a sure and true "help-meet" to Him. She's not only going to be fully qualified to stand with Christ; she's going to know what her place is, and how to completely fill it. As the Bible tells us: being "all one in Christ" is across the board equality, which is another thing sin and even human nature has never let us experience.

That means we actually do have almost nothing of experience to draw from, in order to overcome our inner feelings of unworthiness. So, we have to believe God when He tells us He's made us worthy: and use faith to act upon what we believe. Actually; faith is what we're standing on right now; as we declare our membership in the Bride of Christ; because the only thing we know about this body of people is what we've gotten from the Bible. But, like so many other uses of Faith; one day our faith will become "sight"! It will be manifested in reality! At that point, it will no longer be faith!

Everything we know about God shows us He's chosen a specific time to "rest". All other times He's busy; doing things; always aware and in motion. For us, that means all the ideas we've been given about setting around on a cloud, playing a harp; are just that, ideas! As we've seen in places, some of this study is in trying to look at and understand an existence totally absent of sin. An idea was proposed many years ago: about what humans would do without sin in existence: and it has enough merit for us to include, and look at it here.

"If Adam had not sinned, there would be no sin in existence today". That's what most of us believe; but a deeper look doesn't stand up to that teaching.

The point is, that God's command of "don't eat", applied to any and every human to ever come upon the earth. Do we actually think humanity could have gone on for thousands of years without the curiosity of someone taking us all into the problems Adam brought upon us? Not likely!!

Once again we need to open our minds to something else that needs changing. We have to accept the fact that although it "looks good"; there's been almost *no chance* of this world enduring for long without sin: because sin existed before God formed this world and put mankind on it. But!

Let's go ahead and look at how it "could" have been anyway. In fact, it's even more likely that ***this*** scenario will play out after sin is forever gone; and at a time still in the future.

Without sin: without death or sickness on the world; the growth rate in numbers of humans will quickly get beyond even this earth's capacity to feed and house such numbers: even with "the curse" removed. Basically, there's only one of two possible answers to this problem. One; is to establish some kind of birth control! We've heard that China has such a policy in operation right now: demanding that a husband and wife only have one child.

Two; is to find some way to leave the earth and populate the planets. If we believe that none of the planets are inhabited, that adds a lot of weight to the proposal of leaving the earth: and causing the earth to become the nursery by and through which the galaxies can be populated.

In this picture, we also have the wonder of having direct and personal relationship with God, as the planning is done. So there's no end to the possibilities. For instance:

Someone could stand on the earth, with God along with them, and ask God if it's possible to inhabit and populate a particular star. The awesomeness of this picture is in the fact that God could actually tell that person to use their own mind ability and develop that star any they could imagine. There would be no restriction against drawing from God's power and advice. Neither would it be sin if some mistake was made.

The possibilities of humans, working with God, to build and populate entire worlds isn't beyond reason or imagination. It's an answer to the question of "why are the stars without inhabitants"? It's very likely that God had this idea in mind when He created mankind in the first place.

And it's also a fairly reasonable objective to lay before those who simply can't move out of or beyond physical and material things. We just need to remember that all who will spend eternity with God; are going to have a truly awesome transformation happen in their mind ability and function. And someone 90 times more intelligent than is the greatest of us right now; working with God would surely be able to figure out how to build an entire world society. And this is something one can "imagine' with the restriction of our mind still in place: which is an example of how Holy Ghost can help us. But let's look at something just as important---especially to the Bride of Christ.

In the 19th chapter of Revelation; verses 7-9 is an event called "The Marriage Supper of the Lamb". Where verse 7 tells us *"for the marriage of the Lamb is come, and his wife hath made herself ready".*

First, we want to clarify that Israel is *not* a candidate to be "the wife of Christ.

As we look through the Old Testament of the Bible; we see a primary focus upon the relationship between God and all the members of "the Whole House of Israel". God formed the nation of Israel through Abraham: his son Isaac: and his son Jacob; whom God named Israel. Through obedience, and then disobedience to covenant and worship; this relationship moved back and forth in intensity many times. It was so intense at one point that God declared Himself "married" to Israel. But then---later on, He divorced them because of their sin against Him. It's going to take some "doing" by God: because of His restriction against re-marriage: but at some point; either during or after the Great Tribulation; God the Father will again be joined to Israel in Marriage.

So, with Israel destined to become the wife of God, that takes them out of the picture, as concerns the Wife of Christ. That's what we were looking at when we said it looked like the Body of Christ is the only candidate to become His Bride.

When we look at the Body of Christ; we see one singular organization composed of many members; with us: (mostly The Church): being the body, while Jesus is the singular head. 1st Corinthians 12; 18-31 shows us the *positions of function* in the body. But the entirety of the body is under the authority and instruction of our Head---at least that's the way it's *suppose* to work. If we look behind the public front of any Church, we'll see the faults and mistakes of it's leadership: the first of them being that everyone seems to have forgotten that God never took anybody out of the body and made them part of the head---no matter what position they're called to hold. Also:

Being physically separated from our Lord, and watching a steady decline in reliance on the presence of the Spirit is probably the greatest problem we can find in any Church or Denomination. A problem that will never show up in the union between the Bride and Jesus Christ; no matter what kind of distance separates them; because we will always have that 3 cord bond. We also have a promise in 1ˢᵗ Thessalonians 4; 17 that should take away any worry over separation. This verse tells us that after we meet our Lord "in the air": *"so shall we ever be with the Lord"*.

Because of the power of choice, we can find many areas of "schism" in the Body today. In this case, schism means having a lack of harmony, and working to opposing purposes. Personal agenda and selfish motive are often seen as the cause for schism; but they're still a part of choice.

Because we've already noted that the Bride is going to know how to be "help-meet" for Jesus, this is another difference between the Bride and the Body. We'll never see schism between Jesus and the Bride either! That's unthinkable because it's impossible!

Beyond meeting the needs of the Body, the most important work of this union between the Body and Jesus Christ is the work the Father commissioned Jesus to do. That work is *"to destroy the works of the devil"*!

When we listen to the messages being given in our Churches however; it certainly looks like there's a difference between what God intends, and what the Church now has as a primary focus. Today, the focus of the Church seems to be fixated on what things we **perceive** to be our **needs**: which is also different from what *our needs* really *are*. And even our public prayers have begun to sound like some kind of Christmas "wish list", with God being forced into the position of some great "Santa Clause".

When the time comes for the marriage of the Lamb to take place, the destruction of the works of the devil will be nearly complete.

At least they will be far enough along so that we won't be needed on the earth any longer. But the next time someone asks the question "why hasn't Jesus come for us yet"? Now we have an answer: "the destruction of the works of the devil isn't done".

The greatest difference between the Bride and the Body is most probably in development and growth. As long as we remain on the earth, the Body of Christ is going to continue to need to develop. On the other hand; at the marriage supper of the Lamb, the Bible declares of the Bride; ***"and she hath made herself ready"***! But we also believe that a major part of making the Bride ready, is in developing and maturing this Body of Christ.

Having looked at it: we can probably now agree that removing the restriction upon our minds will take the Body far along in development. But, because it's something we all seem to have overlooked; and failed to include, the removal of restriction upon our minds is going to change or adjust nearly every conclusion we've reached.

What will we know after rapture? How well will we understand the things we're shown that's sure to change? We've been in study with the mind we have right now, and surely in many things we've been looking at the Truth. That will never change! So; with advancement in our mental ability, isn't it going to just be a matter of understanding more depth to these truths we've already discovered?

Because Jesus was sinless, is it proper for us to look at Him, and compare His mental ability to what ours will be? We look at Adam: (before he sinned): and remember that he was so intelligent that he named all the creatures of the earth, as God brought them up to him. And we believe he did it without any other help from God. We can't be sure if Adam used the scientific names for the animals: but calling them cow, horse and pig is pretty astounding if we remember Adam had nothing for reference.

For years; people have "stumbled" over the fact that the Bible declares we will "judge angels". And although we've known that God will have to transform us to a mind level which qualifies us to judge; we didn't think about what that transformation would be; or how high God will have to take us. Now, we have at least a beginning for understanding.

The mind restriction we have upon us, is an answer to many of the questions we've had, about how and why Satan & Co. seem to win so often: especially when we've been so foolish that we tried to meet him without God.

But now we know we've been like a one-legged man in a foot race, and we can tell Satan it's surprising he hasn't been able to do any more against us than he has. Obviously God works in our behalf even when we forget to ask Him. Thank you Father!!

The Legacy of the Church

In the world today; only in 'The Church" do we find people who even try to answer the questions we all have about God; about Jesus Christ; and about the Bible. That's the way it's been for the last 2,000 years: because it's only in the Church that we find Holy Ghost working to help us find the Truth.

Surely, most Christians would agree that the greatest thing we've been able to do for God in these years; is to help bring souls to Salvation found only in Christ Jesus. Probably; as concerns the rest of the things the Church has done; and that have been seen by the world: the distrust we have of one another: our bitter and emotional debates: and the hypocrisy of our lives: all have been a source of some entertainment. And yet unseen by the world; and in the eyes of God; He sees us as though every one of us has been as obedient as Jesus Christ. In a way, that's what we call another "burden of Salvation"; because we feel an obligation to live up to the things God gives us "credit" for being and doing: and know we can't.

No matter what any of us thinks, or tries to tell the rest of us; God is the one who will "judge" the Church! We should be very thankful for that fact: because God is more likely to judge us through Love and Mercy; with His eyes on Jesus Christ; while we would judge through Law and Demand; with our eyes on one another.

But no matter what things we've done; or left undone so far; what we leave behind us: (our legacy): just may be equal to the "great commission" we've tried to live by and obey. Because: since we're the only ones on the earth who have direct access to God's truth; that leaves us being the only ones who can offer hope and promise to people still on the earth after we leave.

That's why we're being given such tremendous insights into God's plans and intents; in these days before we leave the earth.

Although God does have secrets, He's never worked in secret! God has always told people what He's going to do! If he's asked, He will tell us how He does the things He does. And there have been many times when He's said when He was going to do something! As concerns the entirety of humanity: one of the most important things God has ever said is that *"it's not God's will that any should perish, but that all come to righteousness"*! In other words: if God were the only one with a choice in the matter of our eternal future; no one would spend eternity apart from God! O, if only the world would believe this. But to insure an eternity without sin or the devil, God has had to set up the greatest of human powers---*the power to choose*! The authority of personal accountability! And the power of moral responsibility! Satan will never be able to accuse God of being a liar; or failing to submit to His own Law!

Neither will he ever be able to accuse God of "playing games" with this power of choice. He will never be able to say God didn't either give everyone a choice; or else make a provision for those who may have lived at a time which denied them the choice to gain everlasting life through Jesus Christ. That's why it's so important that we find out what God has said to these people; and what provisions He's set up for them after the Church is taken out of the world. And the place where we start; is under the 5th seal of Revelation. Although the seal itself isn't a part of *our* legacy.

In the 4th verse of the 20th chapter of Revelation, we see a group of people who become martyrs for Christ sake by being beheaded. The gruesomeness of their death is "troubling" to nearly everyone, and for any number of reasons.

But as we look through the chronology of events, it's clear that these people are murdered throughout the entirety of the 7 years of Great Tribulation. And with the great change of things, which happens after the "abomination of desolation" it's also clear that the majority of these people die in the last half of Tribulation. Please note: and there's a lot of evidence that lays behind this conclusion.

Because Americans especially seem to have such an abhorrence of people being beheaded by use of a sword: and because it's a fact *they've* been trained to accept: the Muslim radicals: (terrorists): truly believe in and choose to use death through being beheaded by the sword as their primary means of killing people. And because it's such a great way to "terrorize" Americans; these Arab radicals seem to be having a lot of "*fun*" doing it publicly, and in front of a camera.

The point that opens this all up for insight, is the fact that the people who **refuse** and **reject** the "mark of the beast", are the ones being beheaded for Christ's sake. That identifies the users of beheading as being people who are totally in opposition to the real Jesus Christ. In study, we can now also see them being obedient to "the image of the beast"; which is the one who demands the death of those who refuse" the mark"! This also puts them "in league" with the false prophet, who's the one who makes the "image of the beast" in the first place. So; because prophecy of the "end time" is such a popular course of study, we can now and clearly point to the terrorists as being people who will unite with the false prophet and with the "image of the beast".

We've identified the people who are beheaded for Christ's sake. They will be the 3rd phase, or 3rd part of an entire 3 part harvest of people. They're important to us, and to our legacy, because we've only recently seen that God is charging us with a message of "hope" for them; that will continue after we're taken out of the world in rapture.

For the most part, and ever since Christians began to see this great event we call "the rapture"; our lesson to the world has been "now or never"!

Our sermons have been that when this rapture happens: when Jesus comes to gather all the Born Again Christians from the world: the offering of Salvation through Christ will be "taken off of the table"! And we've preached that ; even with the message of "escape through being beheaded" standing squarely in front of us, and for all this time. Basically though, we've either ignored it altogether, or we've chosen to set it aside. And the focus of our message today has become "no hope"; "no hope" after we're gone.

Certainly! There will come a day and an hour when "NO MORE" will be given the offer of eternity with God. That day is NOT the rapture of the Born Again however. For those of us who've come to believe that rapture must come before the Great Tribulation begins; we also have to agree that God has at least 7 years after we're gone, to keep on bringing people into His Everlasting Kingdom. And today; while we're still here, *we* have an obligation to preach this message of hope and promise to those who will still be on the earth when we leave!

That's our legacy! That's our "message in a bottle" we leave behind us! That's the encouragement: That's the promise and hope; of still being offered Everlasting Life with God, that we're to leave for those who come to see what our "calling away" means for them.

In reference to this final message from us; the word that's most often used is "to Overcome"! Jesus Christ has "Overcome" for us! These people, who will still be here after we leave; will have to "Overcome" for themselves! By the way: that's what we mean when we day "becoming one's own sacrifice"!

In the 20th chapter of Revelation; part of verse 4 declares this: ***"and I saw the souls of them that were beheaded for the witness of Jesus, and for the word of God, and which had not worshiped the beast, neither his image, neither had received his mark upon their foreheads, or in their hands: and they lived and reigned with Christ a thousand years."***

We've used this verse already, and we may use it again. Because this is the very essence of our legacy! It's a message to every human who finds themselves still here and present, after the majority of the Church has suddenly disappeared. It's a message that says ***"do not take the mark of the beast"!***

No matter what circumstances of health or welfare they find themselves in; taking this mark means everlasting damnation: without any chance or hope of return to what was!

Our message: our warning: is ***"overcome and resist any and every effort that will lead to taking this mark upon one's hand or forehead!!*** We can't say it any stronger; and neither will repeating it over and over say it any better! As we've also said; we're firmly convinced that the message to "the 7 Churches of Asia" is a message directly from Jesus Christ to these people who will have to resist this force of the devil.

When we're gone, this message from Christ will continue to stand; and continue to be useable as a force and power to "overcome" the mark of the beast! And no matter what debates we now have over whether or not the 2nd and 3rd chapters of Revelation are to these people.

Once again we'll say it: Many people today are confused by this message: because it seems to be saying that it's possible to gain Salvation through "works". Since we believe it to be a message of how to Overcome the force of the Beast: then it also becomes a message of how to gain everlasting life with Jesus Christ; and become members of our Body; through ***this one "specific" work*** of being beheaded!! So:

Even though Christians today have mostly formed unyielding opinions; and stand upon emotional debates: our beliefs and opinions will not change God's word! And because we're **certain** this message is to the people who are to be beheaded for Christ's sake; God's word ***will be*** available to them when the time comes for them to need it!

Security Leads Us Into Freedom

One of the greatest freedoms we have as a Christian; is that we're free to challenge all we're taught; and even all we've come to believe. In fact, if we've associated ourselves with people who try to restrict us from asking questions of their belief system, the chances are we're "in with the wrong crowd". In the fact that God says "come, let us reason together"; it's clear that not only is He inviting questions, He truly wants to hear our opinion; and the body of evidence we've used to reach the conclusions we've come to. Challenging; questioning what we believe is one of the ways to keep it lively and up to date. The worrisome part is that we seem to see fewer and fewer people who question anything they're being taught. And it's either that they don't care anymore, or we're all just "marking time; waiting for the Lord to come and get us. Waiting on God is probably the answer, especially if we all have the same mind set that there's nothing major left to be done until Jesus does come for us.

Once more we declare; there's a Legacy we need to leave behind us!! But we have to know what it is before we can leave it! As we've seen; it's truly an important message of hope, and opportunity for those people who will still be on the earth after we leave in rapture. It says that even though many have rejected Jesus; even after those who are Born Again are gone, God is still offering eternal life with Him. "God's graciousness and desire to gain as many as He can get to fill His Kingdom, sometimes just stuns our mind. But in knowing that as long as the Body of Christ remains on the earth, and God's offer of Salvation through Christ is still open; we feel a security in knowing at least this much of what God is doing.

And usually; when we know what God is doing, we have an almost instinctive desire to "help out": to participate: and to be useful to God in His work. In the Bible it's called "works"!

Actually, wanting to and feeling a desire to "join in", is a sign of having an inner security and peace of mind. Because: It's a part of the "nature" of humans to withdraw and become self focused when we're in pain or stress. That's one of the reasons the devil likes to see us sick or hurt: because he's learned that we do become self focused at those times. It's also why Satan & Co. work so hard to keep us so "busy" we don't have time to study: and if we do force the time, we're usually so tired we can't comprehend what we're reading. This is also one of the "signs" God told us about: that near *the end* people would "become lovers of pleasure more than lovers of God". But: Please note once more:

We've already mentioned that a lot of Christians seem to think there's nothing left for the Church to do before the rapture happens.

After the rapture; we'll be able to look back and see the events that did have to come to pass before rapture could take place! Because we don't have a lot of information about things that are now preventing this great event from happening, maybe our focus is too narrow! Like people in great stress, pain, or sickness, the people of the Church have "narrowed down" our focus to include only the Church. This leaves us overlooking a lot of things that are yet to happen in the world; and which also have a restricting influence upon our rapture. This narrower focus also has us doing something we'd be better off not doing; which is:

The "blinders" we wear, has us looking so intently upon our futures that we fail to enjoy the things that are passing us by. Maybe that needs explaining:

Every one of us has read the back of the book; where it declares "WE WIN"! And if we truly believe "**we win**"; shouldn't we also have a natural "Attitude of Victory"? Actually: we should have confidence and excitement exuding out of us like a light that can't be kept under a box!

In short: when we truly believe "**we win**"; and therefore stop the pressures and pains from robbing us of that part of our Victory; we should really enjoy watching God Win: and participating where we can. God's Victory begins with the declarations of prophecy! And it's a number of Victories that we add all together, as we watch them build into the great and final Victory! It's a "living play", that moves us through the entire spectrum of emotions: from the agony of sadness and loss; all the way up to the mind consuming gladness of glorifying the Victor. That's what we mean as we look to enjoy the events as they happen! That's also the "freedom" we seek; which can only come to us when our confidence and security are solid and sound. Freedom to enjoy God's Victory is something that can only be found in and through Jesus Christ! None, but those who are "in" Christ Jesus will ever imagine such freedom is possible: And none but we who are Born Again will ever gain it!

Security from Knowing our Enemy

In the subjects we've chosen to study; many of the "problems" we have comes from the fact that they're all unsettled disputes! The term "so, we agree to disagree", is how we end much of our study time: which is, to us, about the same as saying "no matter what you say, I don't intend to agree with it"! And the greater disappointment is that we have to wonder if these other Christians are saying they're "not going to listen to God either".

But that isn't an explanation of our enemy! At least we pray God things aren't so bad that some other Christians have now become or enemy. Our true enemy is still Satan & Co.! Plus the many humans working with him; or under his influence; who hate us almost as much as he does!

We've learned that one of the ways to understand some of the things about the devil, is through study of prophecy. Since prophecy is God telling everyone that there are specific events which are going to happen in the future; Satan's response to prophecy is either also fore-told in the prophecy itself, or else we can study how he will most probably respond: and then after the prophecy has been fulfilled, we can study how he did respond. Prophecy seems to be the one subject that's being studied today far more than any other subject we could name. Often times though, when a prophecy is fulfilled and becomes reality, it *still* seems to be as much of a surprise; as is a lot of times when the effort to use Faith *actually* results in what was asked for. Our conclusion on that subject; is that there's so many people publishing their own false opinions and ideas; that those who really don't know *continue* to be confused. The Bible warns us that when the blind lead the blind they both fall into the ditch.

But there's an example of a fulfillment of a prophecy happening right in front of our eyes; and few, if any seem to be picking up on it. Possibly because what is happening doesn't "fit" with the scenarios most have been preaching. But if we really and truly want to find out what our enemy is doing; what we're about to be told is extremely important.

In the 17th and 18th chapters of Revelation, the primary subject is "the city of Babylon. In 18; 1&2, a mighty angel comes down from heaven and declares "Babylon the great is fallen, is fallen. Clearly, this angel is declaring that the city of Babylon will "fall" more than once. And after the "last" fall, the smoke from her burning will "ascend into heaven forever". The problem no one seems to want to look at today, is that in order for a literal Babylon to "fall" this old city must be **rebuilt** in order for it *to* fall in the "last days"! So most are trying to "spiritualize" some kind of non-physical Babylon that will be destroyed. Obviously, no one wants to go along with literal prophecy, and admit that this is the same Babylon that stands in ruins in Iraq this minute.

Well; not entirely in total ruins: because: Before *his* world came tumbling down Saddam Hussein had began a rebuilding program in the old city: Probably thinking to set himself up as another of the Kings who ruled the entire Empire from the city called Babylon the Great.

The major problem our "interpreters of Prophecy" are having with Babylon, is that in the Bible the Prophecy is given in both physical and non-physical terms and pictures. But!

If any have been watching "discovery T. V." lately, these channels are showing tremendous building programs on-going in most of the major "oil rich" nations. It's a lot like Col. Mummar Ggaddafi of Libya: (pronounced like Moammar Kedaphy): who has this wonderful 20 mile 4 lane highway, going out of Tripoli into the desert.

It has a wide center island with palm trees, watered grass, and landscaping. The road surface is so smooth there isn't a bump or dip in it. But! It ends in *a golf course*! There's **nothing** else on it **except** the golf course. No traffic; because it doesn't go anywhere. And no one is allowed to use it but Ggaddafi and his friends and visitors anyway! A waste of millions of dollars? Sure! But that's why it's there---to show everyone that Ggaddafi has so much "oil money" he can waste it, and "flaunt" his wealth in front of the world.

We've noted all this because so much money is available: (Billions and Billions of dollars): for these extravagant building projects in these countries. And so much machinery and manpower is being used that a "high-rise" tower can be built in half the time it normally takes.

The connection we need to make; is that the Bible tells us when Babylon falls the last time, Revelation 18 shows a world wide weeping and mourning *because* of her fall. The description is of a city that's been **totally central** to world wide commerce and trade. That's literal! Not spiritual!! And it's neither imagination nor guesswork, to connect this power and direct focus on world wide economics, with "the mark of the beast": which is shown in Revelation 14; 8-11; because it's all right here in front of us.

When the city of Babylon is restored: (and given what we've seen in the building programs of the other Arab nations; it can be done in a very short time): she becomes the center of almost all world wide commerce; banking; and trade. With the power of that centralization being taken over by the "false prophet; and the image of the beast"!

That's explained in Revelation 13; 11-18; where we're told *"and that no man might buy or sell save he that had the mark, or the name of the beast, or the number of his name."*

The force and power that's going to be in this rebuilt Babylon the Great, is something no one can avoid; but no one seems to know where to put it in the order of chronological events.

And because of that; neither has anyone seen the earthly effect this city is going to have on the 7 years of Great Tribulation. In our studies thus far, the most likely picture we can see, is that the restoration of Babylon the Great is connected to the renewal of the Israelite covenant of Daniel 9.

We can picture a "trade-off" between the "man of sin" and some of the people of Israel; in which this man will trade the "Dome of the Rock" temple; or the area around it; in order to convince Israel to leave him alone while he rebuilds the city of Babylon. For example:

Some of our Muslim friends tell us that the Muslim people are looking for a great Ayatollah to come onto the scene and lead them. The "credentials" they look for, and that this man will hold; are so close to being "the man of sin" and "the son of perdition" that's shown in the Bible; it's beyond coincidence. And such an Ayatollah would have governing power strong enough to override anyone who might oppose him: especially as he contracted and allowed the Israelites to rebuild Solomon's temple. Because:

In order to regain Solomon's temple, there's no doubt but that the Jewish people would allow a restored Babylon the Great to stand, even though it would be a potential threat to them. And if all of this comes into being; the "man of sin": this person we now call "anti-Christ": would gain a "peace" for those who follow him; and "bragging rights" for the same.

In knowing that the "Jew" would be so focused on returning to the "old ways of the Law" they wouldn't be a threat to the things he plans to do; the "man of sin" can declare himself to be a man of peace. There's also another action we believe will involve the man of sin, and the rebuilding of Babylon the Great.

In the 38th and 39th chapters of Ezekiel, is a yet to be fulfilled prophecy concerning an invasion of Israel by a "Northern" coalition of nations. Following the blood line; family relations; and heredity of a people, is far more accurate than trying to follow the movement of nations and peoples. Using that system, those who've done the research teach that the focus of this Ezekiel prophecy is on the majority of what was the old Soviet Union. That this invader: (Gog): is of the blood line of Noah's son who traveled North from where the Arc set. Magog is the land of Gog, and Ezekiel speaks of them being brought down from the Northern parts. This great invading army will also include armies from Turkey; Syria and Iran, which is old Persia. Surprising many: even though this great invader comes out of "the North parts", most of it will be composed of people who hold to Muslim beliefs. Russia for instance, is today nearly 40% Muslim. Please note:

At the writing of this manuscript, fires and drought have been terrible in Russia for many weeks now. So bad is the devastation that just recently their Prime Minister: (Putin): stopped all export of wheat.

Although this may not be God's "timing": (God knows): this is the kind of tragedy that could become the cause for this great army to invade. Because instead of helping Israel defend itself against invasion, the rest of the world stands by and asks the invader "do you come to take a spoil"?

The most glaring question is "where is the United States when Israel is being invaded"? Will we have a leadership so beaten down and sick of years of war in Iraq and Afghanistan they simply turn away? Or will we have a central power secretly and privately sympathetic to the invader? However:

Israel is well aware of this prophecy. Even though they don't honor what we call the New Testament of the Bible; the prophecy of Ezekiel is in their Talmud, and they know exactly what the prophecy says. So they're prepared for the invader. For example:

The only real in country geographic obstacle to this invading army is the river Jordan: which flows down through Israel. Because they know the prophecy, the Israelites have actually laid out pontoon boats: (strong enough to hold tanks and trucks): to aid the river crossing for the invading army. These boats lay on the riverbank this very hour---they've been shown on T.V. and film.

The reason Israel is so confident, is that the prophesy declares only 1 in 6 of the total number of the invaders will be left standing, when Almighty God comes to the defense of Israel! And as Ezekiel says God will bring an overflowing rain of fire; great hailstones; and brimstone down upon this Northern invader. That leaves no doubt in anyone's mind: Almighty God is the "protector" of Israel; and when this army is wiped out, the message of "hands off" will be abundantly clear! But also:

Study of the chronology of the "end time" has left us with the conclusion that this invasion will surely happen just before the beginning of the Great Tribulation. The only thing we can't be sure of just now, is whether or not the invasion will happen before the rapture or after. But also:

Ezekiel 39;6 does warn that God will also send "a fire on Ma-gog, and among them that dwell carelessly in the isles": which opens the door for something else associated.

Actually some will surely argue that the two events should happen at the same time. Because, if that were to happen Satan would be able to explain away the sudden absence of all the people who are Born Again; as a part of the invasion.

The point of this, will be that no matter how hard the Arab nations hate Israel: they're going to stop whatever they've been trying to do!

Because it's clear they're under the protection of God! **That** will make *everybody* set up and finally take notice.

But that's also, and obviously the reason the anti-Christ will want to make an agreement with Israel, instead of trying to fight them over when and where the temple will be rebuilt: and when he can peacefully rebuild Babylon.

Being firmly established under the hand of God's protection, is also why and how Israel is going to demand that all other "religions" leave their country. These 7 years : which we call the Great Tribulation: are going to be Israel's time to finish the earthly kingdom for Messiah when He comes! And certainly, they're going to be working on that, until they see "the abomination of desolation". That's when this "man of sin" steps into the restored temple and declares that he's God; and by heeding Christ's warning, many of them will quickly leave Jerusalem!

The most important thing we've been working to show in this chapter, is what's going to be the work and actions of Satan; the beast; the false prophet; and the image of the beast when this prophecy concerning Babylon is fulfilled.

It's kind of strange that so many people, who don't even believe we'll be on the earth during the Great Tribulation, are so interested in the prophecies about it.

Part of our fascination is surely in trying to establish some certainty about when the rapture will happen. But, we can't take Faith out of that either.

It's also true that when any one of these prophecies is fulfilled, it's going to verify the truth of the things we've been preaching all our lives. And to be justified in what one believes is something we've all wanted.

But we should also accept the fact that just about the time we think we have it all figured out, and we can see which event follows which event: God shows us something we've missed; and we have to start all over again. That's another lesson in "how to enjoy the trip", and stop spending so much time thinking about the end of it. No doubt, seeing and often being touched by these stressful and painful events is something we'd rather not do, if the choice were left up to us. But we can also see these things happen, and ease the pain of them by reminding ourselves that they must happen; and that when it's all completed, "WE WIN"!

In the book of Ezekiel, the Bible tells us that Satan's wisdom is corrupted. It's fairly obvious then, that Satan isn't going to respond to a situation the way he's expected to. In other words: he isn't "normal"; so neither will his response be normal. That's one of the reasons many of us have had so much "trouble" trying to find out why "Satan continues to struggle. A normal person: (even one who has to live with restricted mind ability): can look at all the evidence God puts forth, and reach the conclusion that "the end" is going to happen only when God determines that time to be! And, that it's going to "end" exactly the way God wants; and has prophesied it will end!

But there stands Satan, trying his best to change times and events, because his corrupted wisdom tells him he can. No wonder the prophet insults him so greatly!

The Security of Knowing

In study, we've found that it's possible to have Faith in such strength that one can have the very same feelings of security we seek through study and knowing! We also know there's not all that many Christians with that kind of ability to use Faith. And fewer still who actually know how to use it!

And so: the security we seek is usually only found in study and knowledge. Maybe that's the better lesson anyway; because when we have to struggle to gain something this important, we're better able to keep it in our mind. But!

The red lights of warning; that flash upon the knowledge we gain from the world tells us to be aware of the pit-falls and traps that surround that knowledge. They warn us to filter out worldly knowledge, so that we remove special interest; manipulation; personal and group agendas; and even outright lies. There's only one book in existence that even comes close to being trustworthy: and man and the devil have "messed around" with the Bible so much that we're now in the place where we must rely on Holy Ghost to tell us if something is absolutely true, in some of these "translations". The "average Joe" and the "common man" of a thousand years ago, would probably swear there was no way to corrupt or pollute the Bible. That's exactly what the corrupters and polluters of the Bible would still have us believe! And we tremble in our spirit when we think of what awaits those who have changed the power of the Bible!

The problem in this is that even though there is penalty awaiting these corrupters, the damage they've caused is already done. People are trying to support their belief system with the lies and hidden agendas that were totally false even when they were added to the Bible: or worse yet; taken out of the Bible.

That's another reason it's so hard to find security and stability through knowledge. Again: more reason to need God to help us know what is true! That means:

The greatest problem we're going to have in this day and age is not going to come from lack of knowledge! It's going to come from having a lack of truth! And our lack of truth comes from not knowing how to divide truth from truth; or how to open our minds to Holy Ghost as He gives us nothing but truth. If we'll only find these things of truth; and use them: we'll find them to be dependable ways to establish other truth! It's similar to moving from "a"; to "b"; to "c": provided "a" and "b" are truthful.

And that's where this particular search ends! When we establish the solid ground of true knowledge: and can make these steps from one truth to another.

There is also our security and stability! But it's all established *first* in the truth about Jesus Christ.

As we've declared: there's no compromise, and no manipulation when it   comes to the things God declares about Jesus! It's only been because of the power of "choice" that God's hand has been restrained; as people have rewritten their versions of the Bible: or as others have chosen to remove parts from it. Which brings us face to face with one more truth.

In these instances where we find that people have abused their power of choice; surely we understand there's a penalty involved: especially in the cases where the abuser has done lasting impact upon people who really needed the truth. There's such a gap of time between the damage done and the penalty for it, that fear of punishment doesn't seem to be strong enough as a deterrent to make them stop. So knowing Christians need to be aware! We need to become the "watch-dog! The "neighborhood watch" for Christians *should have* been working for hundreds of years.

Just a personal note:

Our dad taught that it's O.K. to respectfully question God! And that any "belief system" worthy of being believed must not only allow itself to be questioned and challenged: it must actually invite any and all such challenges. In other words: dad taught that the most dangerous "belief system" is the one that won't allow itself to be questioned!

He taught that when God says "come, let us reason together"; it isn't just "hot air" and manipulation. That God actually does want to hear what we have to say about what we believe: That He wants us to tell Him about the body of information we've used, to reach our conclusion. And that not only will God be reasonable and courteous; He won't just altogether verbally destroy us if He disagrees.

The power of choice actually demands that we not only be allowed to hear every form of belief; but that we not be restricted or manipulated as we choose. This is something Satan & Co. are totally guilty of doing, time after time.

After lengthy and careful study: my wife Terri; our sisters Sarah Brown and Wanda Cress agree: with especially this part of dad's teaching. Not always the case with some of the other things he tried to hang on to.

Please understand; that I wouldn't have been able to offer this to you without the special interest of these women in my life; and the involvement of Holy Ghost. He's our source for all Truth!

It's our prayer that this study has been helpful, and has opened your heart and mind to some of the wonder of knowledge and insight about our God and His plans.

Thank you for taking the time to study with us
Dave Church

About Dave Church

I spent 40 years behind the wheel of a Semi: most of those hours in study and focus upon God's word. The insights and truths I learned from Holy Ghost in that time is far more than can be put into one book! Today, I make those lessons available to you.